Teaching Struggling Students

Laura M. Harrison

Teaching Struggling Students

Lessons Learned from Both Sides
of the Classroom

Laura M. Harrison
Ohio University
Athens, OH, USA

ISBN 978-3-030-13011-4   ISBN 978-3-030-13012-1   (eBook)
https://doi.org/10.1007/978-3-030-13012-1

Library of Congress Control Number: 2019932968

Cover illustration: © John Rawsterne/patternhead.com

This Palgrave Pivot imprint is published by the registered company Springer Nature Switzerland AG
The registered company address is: Gewerbestrasse 11, 6330 Cham, Switzerland
Printed by Markono Print Media Pte Ltd

I dedicate this book to all students who find the courage to struggle.

Acknowledgements

I want to thank Milana Vernikova at Palgrave Macmillan for inviting me to write this book, a process that has allowed me to grow as both a writer and teacher. Thanks also to Linda Braus, who shepherded the book through the process with effectiveness and humor. I also want to thank Murali Dharan for his great work on the editing process. Thanks also to those who reviewed the initial proposal and gave incredibly useful feedback. I don't know who you are, but I know that your close attention guided me many times in the writing.

I talked to my own students frequently about my struggling student experience, both when I was having it and when I was writing about it. They were endlessly encouraging, sharing both their own stories of struggle as well as sources that helped me to think about the issues more creatively. This is true of my colleagues as well, so I want to acknowledge my Higher Education and Student Affairs (HESA) community. More specifically, I want to express my gratitude to the following HESA students and colleagues whose expertise informed my work: Joe Carver (online education), Antonique Flood (unlearning), Pete Mather (service learning), and Katy Mathuews (time poverty). Thank you also to Dave Nguyen and Shah Hasan for introducing me to a wealth of literature that shaped my thinking about pedagogy.

I thank my wife, Christy Zempter, for the conversations that helped me to make interdisciplinary connections both while imagining and writing this book. I thank my parents, Dan and Lindy Harrison, for consistently supporting my goals whether they take me near or far. I thank my friends for their genuine interest in the things that matter to me, particularly Chris Bhat, Carey Busch, and Yegan Pillay, who embody the best of the counseling profession both professionally and personally. I know that living a life blessed by continual interaction with people who care about stretching themselves enriches my work. It is in this spirit that I also thank my global conversation partners, Alev Sacak, Birol Sacak, and Heber Da Silva. The chance to meet such thoughtful and adventurous people motivated me to embark on this journey in the first place.

Finally, I thank Reshmi for being such a brilliant, warm, and funny companion on our 15-week trip through introductory linguistics. I may well have failed my first linguistics course had I not had access to both her brain and encouragement. I also thank Gabriela Gaby Castañeda-Gleason and Selikem Gotah for their incredibly generous spirits in both enduring me as a student and allowing me to write about their classes. They taught me so much beyond the scope of their respective courses. They exemplify the best of college teaching and, along with Reshmi, are ultimately why my struggling student story has a happy ending.

CONTENTS

CHAPTER 1

Introduction

Abstract This chapter provides an overview of the book's themes and organization. I introduce my experience as a struggling student and contextualize it in the current discourse on limited learning in higher education. I highlight key literature on the student learning crisis and situate my analysis in this scholarship. I identify the audience for my current work, namely college educators who care about struggling students, but find it difficult to reach them. I argue that researchers have successfully studied student struggle in the big picture, but miss insights that can only be discovered by delving deeply into the details of the student experience. I offer this book as an attempt to fill the gap in our collective understanding of student struggle.

Keywords Student experience · Limited learning · Academic struggle · College teaching · Higher education

We're in a strange moment in higher education. Both scholarly and popular press books on higher education's failings proliferate. There are countless commissions by professional organizations and governmental agencies about what is variously called the student learning crisis, undervaluing of college teaching, and misplaced priorities in higher education. Whether the shortcomings are real or perceived, anxiety about what goes on in college classrooms seems to be at an all-time high.

© The Author(s) 2019
L. M. Harrison, *Teaching Struggling Students*,
https://doi.org/10.1007/978-3-030-13012-1_1

1

It is against this backdrop that I became an undergraduate student in January, 2017. I did not set out to study the student experience. My goal was to earn certification to teach English as a Foreign Language (TEFL) in order to be of greater service to international and/or immigrant students. Trump's recent election inspired me to reflect on ways I could be a better ally to those most threatened by his ethnocentric policies. I decided I would capitalize on my teaching skills in response to the general feeling that we all need to "do something" to combat the xenophobia heightened by the last election.

In both my research and experience working with international students, language challenges emerged as one of the biggest roadblocks to their success (Su & Harrison, 2016). Having moved from the San Francisco Bay Area to Southeastern Ohio, I found myself missing the cultural diversity that comes from living in a major metropolitan area. I gravitated toward our international students, whose research interests and lived experiences began informing my own scholarship in new ways. I was already becoming interested in language learning as the result of helping students to write dissertations in their non-native language. My goal was to gain the formal knowledge I needed to be of greater service to both my university's EFL learners and to set myself up to teach abroad if the opportunity arose.

I achieved this goal to some extent. I did earn the certificate, which I proudly framed and hung in my office. I learned some things that have made me a better teacher to EFL learners now that I can identify patterns and troubleshoot challenges more effectively. I made some meaningful connections and now have three EFL conversation partners with whom I meet regularly.

The process of achieving this goal afforded some surprise learning that I hope will be useful to readers. While I did not intend to study the experience I had as a student, it became evident to me fairly early on that this could be potentially insightful material. While other faculty have gone undercover to study the student experience (for example, Nathan [2006] in *My Freshman Year*), I signed up for my Linguistics classes purely to learn the material. I had no intent to use these classes for research purposes, which allowed me to gain a more authentic student experience since I was there as a student, not as a researcher.

I didn't just gain an authentic student experience, I gained an authentic *struggling* student experience. By *struggling*, I don't mean I got an A- on one assignment because I was too busy with important professorial work to do my homework perfectly. By *struggling*, I mean I got a 67% on my first Linguistics test. I was tempted to tell a story about blowing off the test, but the truth is that the 67% was what I earned with my full intellectual effort. I didn't tell my wife (also an academic) about the 67% for two weeks. After I had decided to write about this experience, I shared the 67% grade with a colleague whose jaw dropped a little in response. I thought about students, both mine and the ones I've read about struggling with imposter phenomenon. I understood their experience more fully after this one grade than in all the reading, thinking, and speaking I've done on the topic. Second-hand knowledge, no matter how good, only gets you so far. Talking *about* struggling students means a lot more now that I actually *became* one.

Purpose

Scholars, pundits, politicians, employers, and other leaders have been raising concerns about what Arum and Roksa (2011) termed the *limited learning* taking place on college campuses. There is little consensus as to the cause of this lack of learning. Some scholars emphasize the faculty side of the issue by focusing on factors like inadequate training to teach (Robinson & Hope, 2013) and/or institutional undervaluing of teaching as opposed to research and grant writing (Boyer, Moser, Ream, & Braxton, 2015). Other researchers focus on student side of the issue, highlighting the role college readiness (DeAngelo & Franke, 2016), inequities in the K-12 school system (Darling-Hammond, 2015), and/or millennial students' short attention spans (Mokhtari, Delello, & Reichard, 2015) play in the phenomenon of limited learning on college campuses.

It is likely that all of the aforementioned factors (and more) contribute to this phenomenon of limited learning on today's college campuses. I caution against overstating the problem; deep and meaningful learning frequently occurs in university settings. I detailed many examples of successful higher education initiatives in my second book, *Alternative Solutions to Higher Education's Challenges: An Appreciative Approach to Reform* (Harrison & Mather, 2015). More personally as a professor who has taught more than 50 classes at 3 institutions, I've had many occasions to witness my students' growth over the semesters we've spent together.

Hence, I do believe the student learning crisis is sometimes overstated and yet, I also know that many faculty and students struggle for some of the reasons surfaced in the aforementioned scholarship. Issues like limited training in teaching and college student readiness are daunting. The research is helpful in naming the problems, but the "recommendations for practice" sections of these articles tend to leave readers feeling overwhelmed. If, for example, I have to wait for the inequities in the K-12 system to be ironed out before my students arrive on campus "college ready," I'm unsure of what I can do in the meantime. So the scholarship is useful in diagnosing some of the issues, but offers little in terms of what we can actually do right now to reach the students sitting in front of us this semester.

The other body of literature which addresses the experience of college teaching is of the inspirational flavor. Parker Palmer (2017) is the most famous of these authors, offering wisdom and motivation based on his experience as a teacher. I find his work very useful for articulating the value of teaching as well as the ideal attitude from which to approach education. Like the more empirical scholarship on teaching, however, this literature views teaching from the 30,000 feet up perspective without much guidance about what to do in the here and now. Also, this work tends to promote student-centeredness; yet, it is written largely from the perspective of teachers.

This issue of perspective is another limit in the current scholarship on teaching. While some authors focus on students and others focus on faculty, few dig deeply into the dynamic interplay between the two. The likely reason is that there are not many opportunities to view the issue from this angle because people are rarely faculty and students at the same time. Here is where I believe that this book makes a unique contribution to our collective desire for more insight into what it would take to truly teach struggling students more effectively.

AUDIENCE

One of the more bizarre aspects of academic life is that so much of it happens behind closed doors. I've had the same colleagues for many years, but I've only seen a couple of them teach. Although observation and feedback have been shown to improve teaching, faculty are sometimes reticent to access these resources due to self consciousness. The fact that faculty receive little to no pedagogical training is likely a cause of this anxiety. The consequence is a vicious cycle where it's difficult to engage in continuous self-improvement. This is particularly true in the current climate where professors face constant criticism, resulting in an understandable level of defensiveness.

Part of what I hope to offer an audience is a path toward improving their teaching practice from the position of an ally. I reject the characterization of professors as cold, uncaring people who kick up their feet once they achieve tenure. Yet, I also know that many faculty struggle with teaching. Teaching is such a complex enterprise that it might be more accurate to say all faculty struggle with some aspect of teaching. My goal is to offer the reader some insight into how the student experience might inform potential strategies for responding to teaching challenges.

I've written three books prior to this one and have to confess that I did not think of the audience as much as I probably should have. With this book, I imagined the audience frequently in the writing process. I imagined people who teach well, who care about their students and are contentious in developing meaningful educational experiences for them. I imagined people who loved school themselves, which is often a powerful motivator for pursuing an academic career. I imagined people who had a hard time understanding why a student would disengage from class, turn in substandard work, or otherwise fail to achieve course objectives. In short, I imagined an audience very much like who I was before I experienced life as a struggling student.

Gloria Steinem asserted that we teach what we need to learn; I would extend that to we write what we need to read. Like most faculty, I was good at teaching good students. These were people I could understand because they were like me as a student. They participated in class and completed assignments correctly. On the rare occasion that they were confused, they asked questions in class and came to office hours.

I estimate these students at about 3/4 of the population I teach. Then there is the other 1/4. Though they comprise a minority of my students, they tend to take up more of my bandwidth. Until I stumbled into the experience of being a struggling student myself, this was a group that was a little foreign to me. They often appeared checked out in class. They rarely asked questions, despite my repeated pleas for students to do so. They almost never came to office hours, even after having received poor grades on assignments.

Although it was fairly subconscious at the time, I can see in retrospect that my thinking about these students fell into the two basic theories faculty often articulate when trying to make sense of this group. We tend to either locate the problem in the students themselves ("Kids today are slackers") or the K-12 education system ("These students are not college-ready"). There is probably much truth in both these characterizations; I've seen my share of students who lack motivation and/or the skills necessary to complete college level work. Yet, what I learned from being a struggling student myself is that the story is often much more complicated than either of these explanations can capture.

I entered my life as a student with both clear motivation and college readiness; yet, I quickly engaged in many of the same behaviors that I see in my struggling students. I didn't ask questions because I was so lost that I didn't know what to ask. It took me a long time to go to office hours for the same reason. I also didn't do these things because I didn't want to stand out, despite being a reasonably well-adjusted middle-aged person without the need to look cool.

As I began to have these experiences, I began to ask, "Is this how my struggling students feel?" Are the behaviors that look like apathy and under-preparedness really more about confusion and embarrassment? Could I be a better teacher to this group of students if I had a better diagnosis of both the problem and what actually helps? The things that helped me to overcome my own issues as a struggling student were not the things I would have guessed would matter. For example, my friend's daughter Reshmi happened to be in the class and the opportunity to troubleshoot challenges with her made an enormous difference in my ability to be successful.

As a result of that insight, I now make more of an effort to have my students share what they're working on in class so that they can help each other out. It seems like a small point, but it turns out that having a community plays a vital role in students' ability to learn. We get very busy as faculty, which can lead to thinking of things like community building as nice, but not necessary. Having the opportunity to experience life as a struggling student has caused me to rethink my priorities as a teacher. I can see now that what might have seemed peripheral to me can be essential from another perspective.

It is this perspective that I hope to offer the reader who may be feeling confounded and/or frustrated by the struggling students in their classrooms. In this assessment-obsessed era, we're too often encouraged to look to mechanistic solutions to this issue. Technology is frequently touted as the answer, often by companies that stand to gain financially. If software were the solution, we would have made greater strides in solving the problem by now (I'll say more about this specific issue in Chapter 5). What we know helps struggling students is human connection, especially with faculty. What I hope to achieve in this book is providing knowledge about what it's like to struggle as a student so that it can inform and enhance that connection.

There have been times when I didn't know what to do with a struggling student. Most often, these are situations in which I've required a student to come to office hours because they didn't complete an assignment correctly, on time, or at all. I dreaded these conversations because I didn't know what to say. As I reflect on these moments, I realize that there was a level of self-centeredness to my anxiety. Part of me resented the student for putting me in the position of having to be the bad guy issuing a low grade or the pushover offering an extension.

Now that I've been that struggling student, I can see the falseness of this dichotomy. Neither the grade nor the extension should be the issue in this kind of conversation. What matters is the student's understanding and that is a highly individual phenomenon only achieved through good rapport, thoughtful questions, and active listening. While these skills require some work (I'll expand on this point in Chapter 6), the good news is that focusing on them liberates us from the bad guy/pushover binary. As professors, we have a much wider range of tools when we shift our focus from what we should do to what our students need.

ORGANIZATION

Chapter 2 provides context for my experience as a struggling student. I describe the autoethnographic process and how it deepened my comprehension of my college experience both past and present. I discuss how I came to understand the role privilege played in by higher education journey and the discomfort that realization caused. I use this experience of sensemaking as a springboard for examining the ways in which struggle created tensions with other aspects of my identity.

In Chapter 3, I describe in depth what struggle looked and felt like for me. I ground an analysis of this struggle in the context of the literature on grit, a current craze in higher education. While grit often serves as a useful concept, I interrogate the limits of this idea that harkens back to a bootstrap mentality. I conclude that mindfulness, metacognition, and empathy ultimately proved more useful to me than grit in facing the shame and fear my struggling student identity triggered.

Chapter 4 focuses on the insights and strategies that helped me to move through struggle. In this chapter, I emphasize the role collaborative learning played in getting me unstuck on several occasions. I introduce my practicum class in this chapter, highlighting the ways it facilitated my movement into deeper learning, partially through the process of unlearning.

The topic of Chapter 5 is my experience in the online portion of the TEFL program. I provide a critical analysis of my experience in the context of the current literature on the impacts of digital higher education. This chapter is not intended to rehash the well-worn debates about technology, but to elucidate the true costs and benefits of online higher education as experienced by one user.

Chapter 6 provides an analysis of how my experience as a struggling student informed my teaching. I detail recommendations for practice with an eye toward pragmatic considerations when attempting to move from theory to application when it comes to enhancing one's teaching. I deal specifically with how to carve out the time it takes to offer the personalized attention needed if struggling students are to succeed.

REFERENCES

Arum, R., & Roksa, J. (2011). *Academically adrift: Limited learning on college campuses.* Chicago, IL: University of Chicago Press.

Boyer, E. L., Moser, D., Ream, T. C., & Braxton, J. M. (2015). *Scholarship reconsidered: Priorities of the professoriate.* San Francisco, CA: Wiley.

Darling-Hammond, L. (2015). *The flat world and education: How America's commitment to equity will determine our future.* New York, NY: Teachers College Press.

DeAngelo, L., & Franke, R. (2016). Social mobility and reproduction for whom? College readiness and first-year retention. *American Educational Research Journal, 53*(6), 1588–1625.

Harrison, L. M., & Mather, P. C. (2015). *Alternative solutions to higher education's challenges: An appreciative approach to reform.* New York, NY: Routledge.

Mokhtari, K., Delello, J., & Reichard, C. (2015). Connected yet distracted: Multitasking among college students. *Journal of College Reading and Learning, 45*(2), 164–180.

Nathan, R. (2006). *My freshman year: What a professor learned by becoming a student.* New York, NY: Penguin Books.

Palmer, P. J. (2017). *The courage to teach: Exploring the inner landscape of a teacher's life*. San Francisco, CA: Wiley & Sons.

Robinson, T. E., & Hope, W. C. (2013). Teaching in higher education: Is there a need for training in pedagogy in graduate degree programs? *Research in Higher Education Journal, 21*, 1–11.

Su, M., & Harrison, L. M. (2016). Being wholesaled: An investigation of Chinese international students' higher education experiences. *Journal of International Students, 26*(4), 905–919.

CHAPTER 2

Privilege as a Blind Spot to Understanding Struggle

Abstract In this chapter, I analyze privilege as the defining context for my experience as a struggling student. As a critical higher education scholar, I had a good understanding of educational inequality prior to my experience as a struggling student. Being a student, however, gave me deeper insight into how privilege mitigates academic struggle. I came to understand the largely invisible ways phenomena like slack, the time wealth that allows some students the time and space to slow down and concentrate, account for discrepancies in students' capacity to overcome academic challenges. I identify how privilege manifested in my educational journey prior to and including my experience in the TEFL program as well as the autoethnographic process that allowed me to discover this finding.

Keywords Autoethnography · Privilege · Slack · Sensemaking · Identity

My identity as a struggling student took place in the context of the Ohio University main campus. I first entered this space in 1991. After a difficult adolescence marked by the prolonged illness and eventual death of my mom, I arrived at college aching to move forward in my life. I was ready to love whatever college turned out to be. I ignored all advice about practicality and selected classes solely on the basis of what interested me. I chose the 24-hour quiet study all-female residential

© The Author(s) 2019
L. M. Harrison, *Teaching Struggling Students*,
https://doi.org/10.1007/978-3-030-13012-1_2

option so I could read and think and be around people who liked school. Unsurprisingly, I found many of the other students who selected this housing option to be highly relatable and thus felt more connected to my peers than at any previous point in my educational experience.

During my freshman year, I mostly went to class and hung out in my dorm listening to the Indigo Girls with my roommate and neighbors. I felt joy in ways that I had not experienced since I was a very young child, before my mom got sick, before kids got mean. Before my first day of college, the happiest I had been was maybe when I was 4 or 5, learning the wonders of reading by day and swimming or sled riding with my family and friends by evening. At 18, I arrived at school truly fearing that my best days were already behind me.

For me, college lived up to all the trope-ish horizon-expanding, eye-opening stuff claimed by university marketing teams everywhere. Ohio University is a highly picturesque campus with a lot of bricks and leaves and open spaces. I still sometimes feel like I'm seeing scenes from promotional materials when I walk past students sitting in the sun on a breezy day. I completed an undergraduate degree in English in 1995 and a masters degree in Counseling in 1998 before finally leaving the university in 2000.

I never lived off-campus during those years because I worked in a variety of housing positions both during and after the completion of my academic work. My post-undergraduate experience was not as idyllic as my life as a student since working in residence halls necessitates actually dealing with the party culture rather than avoiding it. I started working on a career change shortly after completing my masters degree and eventually landed a dream job at Stanford University. I remember the South Green of Ohio University disappearing in my rear view mirror as I headed to California in the spring of 2000. I remember feeling as ready to leave as I had been to arrive.

Then, in 2011, I very strangely ended up back at Ohio University as an Assistant Professor in the Department of Counseling and Higher Education. I had the rare experience of a second first day in this place where I finally do live off-campus in a quiet residential neighborhood. I was almost exactly 20 years older on my second first day in Athens, but some of the feelings were similar between my 18 and 38 year old selves. Working at Stanford and living in the San Francisco Bay Area enriched my experience of this life in too many ways to describe here, but I also felt depleted toward the end of those 11 years. I was tired of feeling like

I never had enough time or money in a place with legendary traffic and high cost of living. As it had in 1991, Ohio University felt like the manifestation of freedom to me in 2011.

I thrived as a faculty member here, feeling a near instant connection to many of the people around me. I easily found both academic collaborators and personal friends, often within the same people. As a result, I racked up a good number of publications and earned tenure early. The fondness I felt for my campus as a student continued to develop as I experienced it in my faculty role. I continue to find personal and professional fulfillment in my life at Ohio University.

THE INTERSECTION OF PRIVILEGE AND NON-STRUGGLE

The way I just told the story of my happy student experience is true. What's also true about my story is that it contains many elements of privilege that I didn't fully appreciate until I started working on this book. For example, it's true that my mom's death was obviously a tragedy that caused trauma in my adolescence. It's also true that my dad's income and insurance benefits allowed me to get the counseling I needed to work through the grieving process. Many young people experience deaths of loved ones, divorces, abuse, and other traumatic experiences without access to support services to help them cope. My family's economic situation allowed me to start college with mental health resources that were unavailable to other students.

Another aspect of privilege I can see more clearly in retrospect is the fairly high degree of college readiness I had when starting college. When the public schools in my area began to deteriorate, my parents had enough money to transfer me to a Catholic school. I enjoyed small classes, personalized attention, and ample opportunity to reflect on my purpose in life, a quality increasingly valued as part of what helps students to persevere through challenges. I also attended high school before the standardized testing craze, which meant that I had teachers who could craft the kinds of creative and interesting assignments that made learning more pleasurable. Because class sizes were reasonable, teachers could assign a lot of writing and offer detailed feedback on it. This preparation proved invaluable during my freshman year of college when many of my peers struggled with their first papers and essay exams.

Mental health resources and college readiness allowed me to start college with confidence. Another aspect of structural privilege that facilitated my completion of college was the good fortune of graduating high school before the erosion of public funding caused tuition to skyrocket. The cost of college has quintupled since I attended in the early 1990s (Clark, 2016). While I was employed during college and on breaks, I did not have to work the kind of hours that detract from students' ability to focus on academics. Today's students increasingly experience what Vickery (1977) called *time poverty*, defined as a person not having adequate time to attend to their responsibilities and maintain their well-being. Higher education leaders tend to think of working students as older, nontraditional students, but contemporary traditional age undergraduates work at the same rate with 71% of all college students being employed and 40% working more than 30 hours per week (Carnavale, Smith, Melton, & Price, 2015; Logan, Hughes, & Logan, 2016).

The privilege I experienced was emblematic of what middle class privilege looked like in the early 1990s. Had I been a member of the proverbial 1%, I would have enjoyed even more privileges like the educational experience and networks afforded by elite institutions. The relatively recent mainstream critiques of gross inequality are eye-opening and important, but they can also inadvertently mask less visible aspects of class privilege. We've grown accustomed to talking about class in extremes, for example, statistics like the richest 3 Americans owning more wealth than the bottom 50% of the country (Kirsch, 2017).

Extreme examples like this obscure differences between people closer on the economic scale. Seemingly small differences like a health insurance plan that includes mental health services can have large consequences, particularly for young people starting out in life. We tend to look at the class level above our own (Reeves, 2018), which absolves us of the responsibility from owning the privilege we experience at our own class level. The point isn't to wallow in guilt, but to be able to see how our own structural advantages might create blind spots in fully comprehending the challenges of struggling students.

I know this blind spot was true for me when I encountered struggling students before I became one myself. Because I never thought of myself as particularly privileged, I didn't fully appreciate just how college-ready I was when I started college. College readiness afforded the obvious benefits like preparation for rigorous academic work, but also softer side benefits like confidence and comfort.

SLACK

One aspect of the privilege I had is what Mullainathan and Shafir (2014) call *slack*, that is, the space in one's life that allows a person to access a greater share of their intellectual and emotional resources. It's easy to be generous and relaxed when one experiences an abundance mentality. In contrast, Mullainathan and Shafir posit that scarcity imposes a mental tax that preoccupies our minds in such a way that our decision-making is compromised. When we live in a constant state of stress with no wiggle room, we tend to make more mistakes because there is such a high price to pay if everything does not go according to plan. As most of us have experienced, panic does not always stimulate the most effective behavior. Whether it's pushing the elevator button repeatedly or cursing at the other drivers, being in a hurry can stifle clear thinking.

While I was not preoccupied with financial concerns as a student in the TEFL program, I did experience a great deal of anxiety as a result of academic struggle, which I will describe more thoroughly in Chapter 3. In retrospect, I can see that it was slack that allowed me to manage this problem. It would be easy to attribute my ultimate success in the class to intelligence or diligence and these factors probably did play some role. We tend to frame students' success or failure in the language of innate challenge or effort, but the concept of slack helped me to see that proclivity as an oversimplification. We all struggle at some point in our lives and it makes a big difference whether we have the space to work through that struggle or have to continue soldiering on without ever getting the time to catch up. As I reflect on my experience as a struggling student, I realize how important slack was in my ability to work through the issues on a deeper level and thus achieve a greater understanding of both the material and ultimately of myself.

Slowing and quieting down mattered much more than I would have predicted. Letting go of the panic, frustration, and desire for control allowed me to quit repeating the strategies I thought should work and delve into more creative problem-solving. For example, one day during the time I was taking my first Linguistics class, I started Googling the beginnings of questions I had (since I was not even at the place where I could articulate a completely formed question yet). In my Googling, I came across a series of videos where instructors from around the world explained the key concepts in my class. While these instructors were not necessarily better than the one I had for class, I could pause the videos and play them repeatedly, which helped some things finally start to make sense.

Many of the books on student learning focus on academically talented students' boredom with college, emphasizing how they play the game rather than engaging deeply with the material. Blum's (2017) anthropological study presented in *I Love Learning, I Hate School* provides a recent example of this genre of works arguing apathy and lack of challenge as what ails contemporary higher education. While gifted, bored students may represent part of the problem, I find it strange they seem so overrepresented in the literature that delves deeply into the student experience. Students whose struggle is more about actual comprehension than boredom are discussed in the scholarship on student learning, but they are generally painted with a broad, decidedly quantitative brush. Their struggle seems to be chalked up to lack of college readiness and/or emotional maturity. The theory is that they either study too little or party too much.

Neither of these variables accounted for my struggle as a student. I was beyond college-ready, motivated, and disinclined to engage in student party culture. I knew how college worked, had plenty of money for the textbook, and engaged in decent study habits (at first, anyway). I listened in class and read the book, but neither of these things helped much once I was in over my head.

As I reflect back on what helped me through the struggle, I realize time played a surprisingly big role. Time wealth afforded some obvious benefits like actual time to complete homework assignments and study for tests. Reflecting deeply on my privileged student experience has surfaced some hidden benefits as well. The primary benefit is difficult to name, but it has the psychological qualities people associate with tinkering. Some have described the advantages of a tinkering mindset in terms of stimulating creative thinking, for example, as in the famous Google practice of giving employees one day a week to work on their own projects. When my conventional approaches to learning the material fell short, my relative time wealth gave me access to the world of tinkering. I talked to my own students with backgrounds in Linguistics, read additional online sources, and played around with the homework, turning over problems in from different angles to see how I could make them make sense in my own mind. When I consider this experience in contrast to the scholarship on contemporary college student life, tinkering seems wildly luxurious.

NAMING NON-STRUGGLE

We tend to examine pain and suffering. In academia, that examination often takes place in the context of a critical approach that allows for the connection between the personal and the political. For example, students who endured bullying as children might come to understand that phenomenon not only a private experience, but one that may have been marked by institutionalized ableism, classism, homophobia, racism, sexism, and/or other forms of structural oppression. Analyzing that experience though a critical lens can both expand one's understanding and provide an opportunity for healing for people who may have been operating under the assumption that the experience was unique to them and/or their fault.

We tend not to examine happiness and ease. There is a logic to this in that scholarly pursuits are nearly always framed around problems. Outside of academia, too, analysis is generally saved for problem-solving rather than digging deeply into the things that are working in our lives. Positive psychology offers a challenge to this paradigm, encouraging us to examine the "bright spots" in our experiences with the goal of leveraging our successes rather than dwelling on failures. Yet, this is a different thing than critically examining the easier parts of our lives and uncovering the privilege that might be contributing to these positive experiences.

The absence of this kind of critical reflection has real consequences for our ability to experience empathy. Erpenbeck and Bernofsky offer a clear and powerful expression of this problem in their 2017 novel, *Go, Went, Gone*. In this work about refugees' experiences seeking asylum, they provide the following meditation on how those living in comfort fail to care about their fellow human beings:

> Could all these long years of peacetime be to blame for the fact that a new generation of politicians apparently believes that we've now arrived at the end of history, making it possible to use violence to suppress all further movement and change? Or have the people living here under untroubled circumstances and at so great a distance from the wars of others been afflicted with a poverty of experience, a sort of anemia? Must living in peace—so fervently wished for throughout human history and yet enjoyed in only a few parts of the world—inevitably result in refusing to share it with those seeking refuge, defending so aggressively that it almost looks like war? (Erpenbeck & Bernofsky, 2017, p. 241)

As I critically examine my comfortable experience of higher education, I recognize the hidden privilege that undergirded my ease. While nowhere close to the proverbial "1%," I nonetheless had many structural advantages going for me when I entered the TEFL program in 2016. I understood that intellectually, having studied systemic inequality in education at all levels. I even empathized to some degree, having worked with struggling students in a variety of capacities and felt genuine care for them. Yet, I failed to grasp how incredibly positively biased my experience of education had been. Hence, I had not fully appreciated what it meant to genuinely struggle within the higher education context.

Kahane (2009) describes this disconnect between knowing something and being able to do something about it in the context of a class he teaches on global justice. He introduces the dilemma of people who consider themselves ethical choosing not to forgo small luxuries in exchange for the money it would take to reduce poverty. He expresses this choice starkly, pointing out that the $.70 we spend to drink a latte over a cup of coffee could purchase a day's worth of oral rehydration salts and a day's food rations. He points out that knowledge of the issue does not seem to change behavior. He raises the counter-intuitive point that heightening emotions about the issue also seems ineffective, describing how many of us simply look away when poverty-stricken children appear on our televisions. It is in this looking away that he expresses insight into the disconnect, positing that it is actually our fear that keeps us from changing. If we really look at the suffering of another human being, we have to change. Taking that first look requires contemplation, a way of being with ourselves beyond both reason and emotion.

Kahane introduced contemplative pedagogy into the course, which resulted in students wrestling more deeply with their own morality. By focusing on dealing with one's anxieties compassionately, students developed the tools they needed to quit looking away. As Kahane articulated, "They tended to move toward a willingness to experiment with their own tolerance for letting in others' suffering, and with what this might feel like in action" (p. 57). Students began to express that action less in terms of daunting sacrifice and more as an opportunity to achieve greater purpose in their own lives.

Kahane's work resonated with my experience struggling student identity. Although the issues he examines are more extreme, I could relate to the desire to run from distress. It's an understandable reaction, but ultimately one that has to be confronted in order to move forward. I found

Kahane's scholarship insightful for the way in which it highlighted the importance of teaching students to tolerate the uneasiness that inevitably accompanies true growth. My initial impulse with the discomfort I experienced in my first class was to look away, to hide my first test score, to drop the class, to not claim the identity in any way. It was only through contemplation that I found a way to face the struggle and let it transform me into a more empathic teacher.

My Autoethnographic Process

As I shared in the introduction, I did not set out to study the student experience. I enrolled in classes purely to learn the material with the goal of earning my certificate to teach English as a Foreign Language. Perhaps arrogantly, I did not anticipate the courses being too difficult. Classrooms are friendly spaces for me, so I approached my first class more as a pleasant hobby than something I thought would be particularly challenging.

I quickly became aware that I had miscalculated the situation. As early as the second week, I could see that the material was going to be more difficult than I had guessed. I revised my expectations, reconceptualizing the experience as a personal growth opportunity. I still wasn't taking it that seriously, figuring I had the intellectual prowess to persevere. I did start taking some notes on my life as a student at this time, more for the purposes of sharing them with my own students. I was teaching a class on teaching that semester, so my life as a student gave me good stories to share in class.

The first two weeks of my first class gave me interesting material for my own classes as well as my personal life. I enjoyed the first couple of homework assignments, finding it enriching to work on something outside my own field. It was a novelty to be a student again. I posted a lot of warm words about the joy of learning on social media during those weeks. Then things took a dark turn in Week #3 when course content that had once been an interesting challenge became utterly confusing.

By Week #4, I had taken my first test. My score was 33.5/50 or 67%. My first impulse was to drop the class. I was so embarrassed that I couldn't even admit to myself that I was embarrassed. Before my conscious mind could process the 67%, my subconscious had handled the mess by creating a plausible explanation which was something along the lines of, "Clearly you are too busy for this nonsense. This was a nice idea, but you have more important things to do. Drop the class, tell your friends you didn't have time to complete the course, and go back to your life where you feel smart and competent."

Though my first impulse was indeed to drop the class, I could tell that I was onto something here. I was probably not going to make a mid-career change and become a world-class linguist, but I was accessing a world of thought and emotion that had been fairly foreign to me. It's not that I had never struggled in a class before; in fact, I failed high school geometry. But I didn't care about high school geometry, so that was of little consequence. I had limped along in the statistics classes required of my various degrees, but those courses were simply a means to an end to me.

This 67% was different in so many ways, which I will detail later in this chapter. For now, what matters about the 67% is that it led me to decide to start studying my experience as a struggling student. Autoethnographers write themselves into a story, as I have done here. As Denzin (2013) points out, "Narrative texts freeze events and lived experiences into rigid sequences" (p. 35). Though I tried to stay as true to the experience as possible, this text represents that artificial construction by repackaging messy phenomena into a linear sequence. Though this is a necessary process for readability, it's important to be explicit about the fact that what may read as objective reporting at times is the result of countless choices. For example, I chose to start on the first day of class because that seems logical, but I could have begun at the application process or even earlier.

First Day

I arrived ridiculously early, despite having spent the past several minutes trolling for parking. I walked into the empty classroom and reminded myself to sit in a student desk because I was not the professor. I scanned the thirty or so possibilities, all of which were available to me as the first person in the room. Despite years of trying to get my own students to move to the front of the room, I went for the back corner near the door.

I felt a little surprised that the need to escape factored into my seating choice, but I couldn't delve too deeply into self-analysis because my thoughts were interrupted by another student entering the room. He went straight for the front, same row as me. As he passed, he acknowledged me with a head nod, then sat down and immediately began to unpack his backpack. 'I should do that, too,' I thought, copying him and starting to feel a little dumb and self-conscious that I had literally been staring at the wall when this young man came in. Other students started to arrive and all of them managed to at least look like they were doing something, mostly on their phones. They were eerily quiet for a group of young people. I remembered college being louder.

I noticed the light come on in the room, then the instructor walked swiftly toward the front though he was not late. It struck me as funny that we all sat there in the dark until he arrived. I make fun of my students for the same behavior, yet it turns out I do the same thing as a student. The instructor turned on the computer, rubbing his hands up and down his arms while he waited for it to boot up. Most of the students in the room still had their coats on due to the lack of heat. It was January 9th and we were in Ohio, so heat is pretty essential. But as it turned out, we wouldn't have heat in our classroom for most of the semester.

The instructor appeared both surprised and delighted to see his title slide pop up on the screen. He introduced himself, inviting us to both call him by his first name (Selikem) and to let him know if we couldn't understand him due to his accent. He told us that he sometimes has a hard time understanding certain accents as well and, by the end of the course, we would understand more about that. He told us he was a grad student in Linguistics. He apologized for the lack of heat and let us know he'd be looking into that problem.

He passed out the syllabus, which was pretty standard fare. Instructor contact information, course policies, etc. I flipped to the back page and scanned the schedule of classes, noting there would be tests. Yikes! I don't know why this came as a shock, but it did and I immediately started calculating how many years it had been since I had taken a test. 'Let's see,' I thought, 'I'm sure my doctoral program was all papers, so certainly not since 2002…did I take tests as a masters student? I don't think I did, but even if it's not all the way back to undergrad, the last time I took a test was not in this century.'

As I was contemplating what it would be like to take a test after not having done so for literally decades, I realized that I missed the instructions for what I was supposed to do with the index cards the instructor had just distributed. Without realizing it at the time, I did a quick scan of the students nearby and selected the one with whom I felt the most comfort. I skipped over the bro-ish seeming guy to my immediate left, and went for the lefty looking guy to my front-left. "Hey," I whispered,

"What did he say to do with this?" "I think he said he wants our names and one fact about ourselves," he answered politely. "Thank you," I replied, squelching the urge to explain that I was distracted, not too old to hear the directions. I vowed not to get lost in reflection again, a vow that was broken almost immediately after I made it.

All of what I just described here happened within the first ten minutes of the class and it's just a fraction of what I could have written. As I reflect back on that first day of class, I'm surprised by the richness of the experience. I've been walking into classrooms for the past ten years without noticing anything at that level of detail. I have a lot of my mind when I enter that classroom space as a professor, especially on the first day when I'm trying to make sure the technology works, learn students' names, and do all the other things necessary to get off to a good start.

These things are important and need to be done, but my experience of being a student showed me that there was a whole emotional reality to which I had been fairly blind. For example, I was surprised by my instinct to look for the person most like me when I needed to ask a question about the first day icebreaker. I would not have predicted that I would have cared about identity considerations, but my instinct clearly was to choose the person I deemed most similar to myself. I also wouldn't have guessed that I would be inclined to stereotype people, but I definitely did on this occasion and others.

Becoming conscious of this impulse in myself has given me fresh empathy for students whose scan of a classroom yields no other student with whom they feel some similarity. Although I noticed that nearly every student in the room appeared to be white, I didn't really think about the significance of this point until reflecting on how easy it was for me to locate a person with whom I felt some commonality. Many would argue that expanding beyond one's comfort zone and interacting with people different from themselves are important functions of college; this is undoubtedly true. I would argue that this is easier said than done, especially if students don't have a baseline of easy connection from which to draw strength when the challenges of interacting across difference become overwhelming. Intellectually, I understood this idea long before I was a student in my first Linguistics class. Yet, I didn't fully appreciate the deeper meaning of it until I both witnessed and reflected on my own bias toward sameness as a source of stability in a situation where I felt a little unsure.

Denzin (2013) explains this phenomenon of surfacing a hidden reality in the context of the instability of both experience and self as concepts: "Experience, lived or otherwise, is discursively constructed. It is not a foundational category. There is no empirically stable *I* giving a true account of an experience. Experience has no existence apart from the storied acts of performance" (p. 2). Hence, my ability to access the student experience had been extremely limited since that was not the experience I perform as a professor. The opportunity to perform my student *I* gave me a deeper, richer understanding of that phenomenon than I could have achieved in any other way.

WHY AUTOETHNOGRAPHY?

We are in a Catch-22 of sorts when it comes to deepening our understanding of how students experience education. If we're only comfortable with what can be measured on a test, this method will drive us toward research questions that can be answered in this manner. Research that is generalizable, reproducible, and fundable tends to require approaches that are reductive in nature. The result has been a partial understanding of how students learn. While traditional methods provide important insights into the student experience, they often require a reductivism that renders the aforementioned interconnections invisible. It is difficult to examine a phenomenon holistically with methods that require researchers to isolate variables.

Shahjahan (2005) explains this reductivism in the context of universities' emphasis on individualistic competition in this era marked by academic capitalism. When education becomes a largely vocational means to a narrowly financial end, topics that do not lend themselves to positivist frameworks become marginalized. As Shahjahan explains, "This trend reinforces the empirical and ideal nature of knowledge production, and therefore what is invisible and has no visible or material impact is not considered worth studying" (p. 693).

The result is that we are stuck in our quest to understand how students experience learning. Autoethnography creates the possibility for an in-depth, holistic analysis of a phenomenon. It allows for a blurring of line between researcher and researched. While there is a robust scholarship on student learning rooted in both quantitative and qualitative methods, this literature is limited by its focus on students as objects of study.

A firm line between the researcher and the researched can lead to literature that reports, but doesn't necessarily elucidate. Jones, Adams, and Ellis (2013) illustrate this point effectively in their introduction to the *Handbook of Autoethnography*. They discuss the limits of conventional researchers who can unwittingly objectify and/or exoticize the other in their attempt to maintain distance from those whom they research.

Jones et al. (2013) posit that this distance often makes for sterile scholarship devoid of the potential richness of the experience under investigation. They use Walker's (2009) essay, *A Feminist Critique of Family Studies* as an example. In this work, Walker writes of editing a journal about family issues while experiencing health crises in her own family. She felt pressured to stick to writing impersonal academic essays, squelching the insights she was having through her lived experience. She eventually began incorporating these experiences as well as calling for pieces that encouraged other authors to do the same.

The aforementioned process is referred to as reflexivity; that is, awareness of and accounting for the researcher's role as an instrument in the research process. Reflexivity is used as a safeguard against bias or, more accurately, as a process of self-reflection that allows researchers to surface their prejudices in order to minimize their influence on the research. Hence, reflexivity plays a vital role in qualitative research in that it shows how the researcher's experience of a phenomenon informs their approach to it. Reflexivity is part of what allows for the deeper understanding Walker's (2009) work exemplified.

In short, the desire to understand the student experience more holistically and the motivation to neither objectify nor exoticize another led me toward autoethnography. This notion of being led provides another aspect to my specific experience in terms studying a phenomenon I did not intend to study.

Epiphany

Identities are cultural creations with names that are attached to persons, such as *only child* or *woman* (Denzin, 2016). While these identities feel static, their meanings can change in various contexts. Similarly, the significance of these identities is also context-dependent. One's gender identification, for example, might matter little or not at all when buying a cup of coffee but takes on greater significance when buying clothes.

Autoethnographies are built around epiphanies, which Denzin (2016) defines as effects on identity that "cut to the inner core of the person's life and leave indelible marks on him or her" (p. 130). These effects are necessarily disruptive, causing a person to question a core part of their identity. Epiphanies involve surfacing taken for granted assumptions about who we are. These assumptions are normally hidden because our performances of our various identities feel so natural that we engage them automatically.

Denzin (1984) explains this enactment, "Within and through their performances, persons are moral beings, already present in the world, ahead of themselves, occupied and preoccupied with everyday doings and emotional practices" (p. 131). We go through our days with little awareness of many of our identities unless something happens to surface them. When an experience raises our consciousness about an identity and causes us to question and/or examine it in a new light, the result is an epiphany.

In my case, I did not realize I had an identity as a "good student" until I became a struggling student. The most obvious issue is that I was not, in fact, a student until I enrolled in the TEFL program. Yet, the experience of failing my first Linguistics test was an epiphany in that it did cut to the core of this good student identity I realized I had once it was threatened. Part of what made the 67% an epiphany for me was reflecting on how I kept that grade a secret. I knew that I would have responded differently to a failure in my life that meant less to me.

When I went through a period of locking my keys in my office, for example, I shared those stories as humorous anecdotes. More importantly, I sought help for getting back into my office, expressed appreciation to the person with the master key, and developed strategies for avoiding this problem in the future. My lack of identity as a Responsible Key Owner, allowed me to address that issue head-on and resolve it (for the most part). In contrast, the bad test grade disrupted my Good Student identity so thoroughly that it left me somewhat incapacitated. This disruption laid the ground for an epiphany that has helped me to make sense of the seemingly illogical acts of self-sabotage in which struggling students frequently engage.

Good students become good professors, an identity I performed through working hard, producing publications, teaching well, and earning tenure. As I reflected on this identity, it occurred to me that school had always worked out for me from preschool through my doctoral program. It's not that I never had a hard class or challenging assignment, but I had operated within my comfort zone in terms of subjects I deemed myself "good at." Additionally, I had a deeper awareness that the education system was basically made for me given my white, middle class identities.

I did not know how to be a struggling student because I did not know how to perform in the context of this identity. My good student performance of working hard, sticking to a schedule, etc. did not particularly help my struggling student self. My discomfort in being a struggling student exacerbated the situation because I wanted to shed that identity as quickly as possible by succeeding in the class. Part of my epiphany in this process was realizing that my good student performance strategies were not necessarily going to work, at least until I admitted this struggling student identity and dealt with it.

The Need for Sensemaking

Higher education takes place within an organizational context that warrants examination. The concept of sensemaking serves as a useful lens through which to examine the dynamics that comprise one's experience within an organization. As Weick, Sutcliffe, and Obstfield (2005) explain, "Sensemaking involves turning circumstances into a situation that is comprehended explicitly in words and that serves as a springboard into action" (p. 409). Sensemaking entails what its name suggests in terms of allowing people to understand the selves they experience against the backdrop of the various social, cultural, and political contexts they encounter everyday. Through gaining a deeper understanding of the co-creation of self and context, individuals have the potential to gain greater agency in their lives, hence the emphasis on action.

Roberts employs the action orientation of sensemaking in her work, *Negating the Inevitable: An Autoethnographic Analysis of First Generation College Student Status*, emphasizing "giving agency to other FGC (first generation college) students" as her motivation for writing the piece (p. 59). She juxtaposes her personal story of being a first generation college students with the prolific research documenting the ways in which this group possesses lower social capital, receives less parental encouragement, understands financial aid inadequately, and drops out of college at higher rates than their continuing generation counterparts. While good motivations often undergird this scholarship that does play an important role in identifying trends, it necessarily operates in broad brushstrokes.

Weick et al. (2005) point out the limits of focusing on trends to the exclusion of the smaller picture, a rich source for sensemaking at a deeper level:

...the order in organizational life comes just as much from the subtle, the small, the relational, the oral, the particular, and the momentary as it does from the conspicuous, the large, the substantive, the written, the general, and the sustained. To work with the idea of sensemaking is to appreciate that smallness does not equate with insignificance. Small structures and short moments can have large consequences. (p. 410)

Roberts (2014) describes one of these "small moments" in her experience of attending office hours after receiving a low grade on an assignment. The professor states his frustration with students like her who have transferred to his private university from community colleges he feels provide "inadequate education" (p. 56). Roberts shows how his familiarity with general trends rather than specific students limits his ability to communicate with her. She points out that he could have asked questions about her unique path to his classroom, "but instead, he relied on stereotypes" (p. 57).

Roberts could have made sense of this experience in a variety of ways, all of which were potentially consequential to her success as a college student. Although she lost some confidence after the aforementioned experience, she regained it in subsequent courses. She gained knowledge that empowered her to address her "tarnished self" and "led me to a path of healing by lending me theoretical language to explain my experiences" (p. 58).

What happens to students who don't have access to alternatives to the tarnished student identity? In the absence of theoretical tools to understand selves as constructed and therefore mutable, students are likely to internalize that proverbial fall from grace. I know I've seen it countless times with my own students who assure me that they are irredeemably bad writers. Now I make it a point to tell students that no one is born a good or bad academic writer, that it's sheer practice that builds skill. I'm continually amazed by how much this revelation often means to students, particularly those who have been told they simply lack talent.

THE ROLE OF IDENTITY IN LEARNING

While Roberts identified as a confident student after having succeeded at her community college and acquired academic awards, her ideas about her self changed in the new context of her private university. The office hours experience that led to the creation of Roberts' "tarnished self" exemplifies Yep's (2002) notion of identities as co-created in daily life.

Students need theoretical tools to help them identify the emergence of selves in the university context, particularly those with a "tarnished" element that can be corrosive to their ability to thrive. My experience of getting a 67% on my first test constituted an experience reminiscent of Roberts' sense of being tarnished. I did not want to go to class the next day, nor did I want anyone to know that I was a failure. I did not think of the failing in behavioral terms, as something within me. I most definitely conceptualized the failure as a new identity of sorts, one that did not necessarily eclipse my previous academic successes, but one which did call them into question.

I would never have gotten to the word, *tarnished*, without Roberts' autoethnography. When I tried out the word, *tarnished*, on my own students, it resonated more aptly than any other descriptor I've used when teaching about the college student experience. My students began speaking animatedly, bravely, and vulnerably about times they felt their own academic accomplishments had been tarnished by experiences in their own lives. They frequently attributed their ability to employ sensemaking with regard to those experiences as integral to recovering and moving on.

How often do we create experiences that allow students to engage in sensemaking with their own struggles? Too often, we advise them in terms of actions: go to the tutoring center, drop the class, change your major. We don't spend enough time asking thoughtful questions about the process of students' learning. If the self a student is constructing in a given moment is one that is tarnished in some sense, advice might address symptoms rather than causes. Worse, advice can disempower by promoting general formulas rather than acknowledging students' individual struggles within the contexts that shape them.

IDENTITY SAFETY

I've read countless accounts of how higher education is to a large extent structured around white, middle class culture, but I never really understood that very deeply until I had the experience of being a struggling student. Though slogging through difficult material wasn't fun, I did not experience the phenomenon Steele and Aronson (1995) termed, *stereotype threat*. Stereotype threat is "being at risk of confirming, as self-characteristic, a negative stereotype about one's group" (p. 797). Steele and Aronson conducted experiments demonstrating a connection between anxiety about the perception of one's minoritized identity and academic underperformance. While I certainly experienced anxiety on test days in my class, I never felt the added pressure of anyone connecting my performance to my race or class identities. My individual "good student" identity floundered, but I experienced identity safety in terms of the relative privilege of my demographic identities.

The literature is replete with accounts of minoritized students' plights navigating higher education, but very few works detailing what privilege looks like in action. I have argued elsewhere (*Interrupting Class Inequality in Higher Education: Leadership for an Equitable Future*, 2017), that the next frontier in the fight for educational equality is to examine social justice issues from the privileged side. Although Nader (1972) identified this issue decades ago in *Up the Anthropologist: Perspectives Gained from Studying Up*, scholars continue to focus disproportionately on the marginalized side of the privilege issue. Nader posited greater empathy for and access to less powerful people as the most salient reasons for this imbalance. One negative consequence to this imbalance is that the resources of the privileged often remain concealed, making it easier to view the disenfranchised from a deficit perspective.

At the Intersection of Resource and Struggle

Perhaps the most significant epiphany I experienced in my sensemaking process of life as a struggling student is that privilege mitigated that struggle in countless ways. My initial reactions to this fact were characterized by a desire to hold this awareness at a distance. I denied, repressed, diminished, laughed off, and then finally opened myself up to the possibility that privilege not only played a role in my experience, but actually defined it to some extent.

These responses echo many of DiAngelo's (2011) points about white fragility. As she points out, we use "racially coded language such as 'urban,' 'inner city,' and 'disadvantaged' but rarely use 'white' or 'over-advantaged' or 'privileged'" (p. 55). The education discourse is no exception in that we talk easily about "disadvantaged" or "at risk" students without acknowledging that the other side of that equation causes the unequal playing field in the first place. Absent a deeper understanding about the role privilege plays in the lives of some students, it's easy to even inadvertently locate the problem of struggle in the marginalized students themselves. Uncovering and facing my own over-advantaged experienced helped me to surface the hidden benefits afforded by slack and identity safety.

At its best, autoethnography can help a person see more clearly both what they are experiencing as well as the what they are omitting or screening out. In terms of the latter, it is notoriously difficult to see what we don't see, to know what we don't know. There is a robust literature on the mind's stubbornness in even noticing what it doesn't expect to see. This phenomenon is called confirmation bias; it occurs because our minds have evolved to focus on patterns and dismiss outliers. In terms of evolution, this peculiarity of the mind is a good thing when it comes to quickly identifying potential food sources, but it proves to be a problem when asked to consider what it deems to be contradictory to its own understanding of something.

Confirmation bias is perhaps why white liberals sometimes seem particularly resistant to an honest examination of racism. As DiAngelo (2011) explains, "If white children become adults who explicitly oppose racism, as do many, they often organize their identity around a denial of the racially based privileges they hold that reinforce racist disadvantage for others" (p. 64). Coupled with invisibility about the specific benefits afforded by privilege, confirmation bias creates a sense of plausible deniability about one's own unearned advantages. This can be an incredibly difficult and painful reality to face; I know my own students and friends generally prefer to talk about the marginalized aspects of their identities more than the privileged ones. I am no exception, but at least I can see it now, not as an abstraction, but in the real and material ways my privilege mitigated my experience as a struggling student.

Conclusion

Despite years of teaching classes with social justice content, it came as a surprise to me that privilege played such a large role in my experience as a struggling student. I would never have guessed that privilege would emerge as the defining theme in my analysis, but I cannot deny that my high degree of access to resources mitigated the challenges I faced. If I hadn't been so steeped in the detailed note-taking required of this kind of writing, I would have told a less complicated story about my experience of student struggle. That story probably would have featured my great perseverance, which could have caused me to feel less empathy for my own struggling students because it would have been easy to conclude that if I can do it, they can do it. There is some truth in this idea, but it's an oversimplification without the acknowledgment that privilege and marginalization create wildly stratified contexts in which students experience higher education.

References

Blum, S. (2017). *"I love learning; I hate school": An anthropology of college.* Ithaca, NY: Cornell University Press.

Carnevale, A. P, Smith, N., Melton, M., & Price, E. W. (2015). *Learning while earning: The new normal.* Georgetown University Center on Education and the Workforce. Retrieved from https://cew.georgetown.edu/wp-content/uploads/Working-Learners-Report.pdf.

Clark, K. (2016, October 26). College prices hit new record highs in 2016. *Money Magazine.* Retrieved from http://time.com/money/4543839/college-costs-record-2016/.

Denzin, N. (1984). *On understanding emotion.* San Francisco, CA: Jossey-Bass.

Denzin, N. (2013). *Interpretive autoethnography* (Vol. 17). Thousand Oaks, CA: Sage.

Denzin, N. (2016). Interpretive autoethnography. In S. H. Jones, T. E. Adams, & C. Ellis (Eds.). (2013). *Handbook of autoethnography* (pp. 123–143). New York, NY: Routledge.

DiAngelo, R. (2011). White fragility. *The International Journal of Critical Pedagogy, 3*(3), 54–70.

Erpenbeck, J., & Bernofsky, J. (2017). *Go, went, gone.* New York, NY: New Directions Books.

Harrison, L. M., & Hatfield Price, M. (2017). *Interrupting class inequality in higher education: Leadership for an equitable future.* New York, NY: Routledge.

Kahane, D. (2009). Learning about obligation, compassion, and global justice: The place of contemplative pedagogy. *New Directions for Teaching and Learning, 2009*(118), 49–60.

Kirsch, N. (2017). The richest 3 Americans hold more wealth than the bottom 50% of the country, study finds. *Forbes.* Retrieved from https://www.forbes.com/sites/noahkirsch/2017/11/09/the-3-richest-americans-hold-more-wealth-than-bottom-50-of-country-study-finds/#626d98043cf8.

Logan, J., Hughes, T., & Logan, B. (2016). Overworked? An observation of the relationship between student employment and academic performance. *Journal of College Student Retention, 18*(3), 250–262.

Mullainathan, S., & Shafir, E. (2014). *Scarcity: The new science of having less and how it defines our lives.* New York, NY: Henry Holt and Company, LLC.

Nader, L. (1972). *Up the anthropologist: Perspectives gained from studying up*. Berkeley, CA: U.S. Department of Health, Education & Welfare (ERIC Document Reproduction Service No. ED 065 375). Retrieved from October 12, 2017, from EBSCOHost ERIC database.

Reeves, R. V. (2018). *Dream hoarders: How the American upper middle class is leaving everyone else in the dust, why that is a problem, and what to do about it*. Washington, DC: Brookings Institution Press.

Roberts, T. (2014). Negating the inevitable: An autoethnographic analysis of first-generation college student status. In R. Boylorn & M. Orbe's (Eds.), *Critical autoethnography: Intersecting cultural identities in everyday life*. New York, NY: Routledge.

Shahjahan, R. (2005). Spirituality in the academy: Reclaiming from the margins and evoking a transformative way of knowing the world. *International Journal of Qualitative Studies in Education, 18*(6), 685–711.

Steele, C. M., & Aronson, J. (1995). Stereotype threat and the intellectual test performance of African Americans. *Journal of Personality and Social Psychology, 69*(5), 797–811.

Vickery, C. (1977). The time-poor: A new look at poverty. *The Journal of Human Resources, 12*(1), 27–48.

Walker, A. J. (2009). A feminist critique of family studies. *Handbook of feminist family studies*. In S. Holman Jones, T. Adams, & C. Ellis Jones (Eds.). (2013). *Handbook of autoethnography* (pp. 18–27). New York, NY: Routledge.

Weick, K., Sutcliffe, K., & Obstfeld, D. (2005). Organizing and the process of sensemaking. *Organization Science, 16*(4), 409–421.

Yep, G. (2002). Navigating the multicultural identity landscape. In J. Martin, T. Nakayama, & L. Flores (Eds.), *Readings in cultural contexts* (pp. 60–66). Mountain View, CA: Mayfield.

CHAPTER 3

What Struggle Feels Like

Abstract In this chapter, I delve into what it feels like to struggle academically. Prior to struggling myself, I tended to overemphasize the intellectual aspects of my students' challenges. This unbalanced approach gave me an incomplete understanding of how the affective dimensions of struggle manifest in ways that appear illogical. For example, I did not understand my students' reticence to seek help until I experienced my own impulse to hide after receiving my first low grade on a test. This chapter focuses on the emotional side of struggle in hopes of shedding light on why students do seemingly irrational things when faced with academic challenges.

Keywords Fear · Empathy · (Critique of) grit · Neuroscience · Metacognition

In the last chapter, I detailed how I came to understand my non-struggling student in the context of privilege. I grew up in a safe home, attended a good high school, and experienced college as an enriching experience that prepared me well for adult life. I graduated on time and debt free. Some of these positive experiences can be attributed to personal qualities, but the larger societal structures that set me up for success undoubtedly played a large role in allowing me to nurture those qualities.

© The Author(s) 2019
L. M. Harrison, *Teaching Struggling Students,*
https://doi.org/10.1007/978-3-030-13012-1_3

This context was also at play in my struggling student experience 20 years later and did mitigate it to a large extent. For example, I had time to focus on my studies, knowledge about office hours and other resources, and connection to a study partner. Some of my psychological resources, however, turned out to be less solid in the face of struggle.

Struggle came as a surprise because the first two weeks of my first Linguistics class were almost joyful. It was fun to be a student again; I enjoyed the new rhythm my morning class brought to my Mondays, Wednesdays, and Fridays. I liked walking into a classroom and not being in charge. I wrote many social media posts about the genuine wonder I experienced as the result of learning things like the following:

1. There are about 7000 languages in the world.
2. Language is a creative system. Language is created, not memorized.
3. There are systematic constraints that serve as a check on the creativity of language. For example, a new verb is rarely coined if a word with the intended meaning already exists.
4. Time expressions that indicate points in time cannot be used to create new verbs. For example, we may say she vacationed, but we wouldn't say he nooned.
5. All languages have a grammar. All grammars are equal.

These are some of the notes from my second day of class on January 11, 2017 (the first day was taken up with awkward icebreakers, so I have no notes from that day). The second day of class, however, was what I had hoped it would be like to be a student again. I was riveted by learning this basic knowledge about language. I remember thinking throughout the rest of the day about how fascinating language is. I was mesmerized by the idea that I use language everyday, yet know so little about it. I read ahead in the textbook and looked forward to the next day of class. I also got online and started to look at other courses I might like to sample once I completed the TEFL program.

The third day of class, January 13, 2017, was not quite as exciting as we delved into the details of phonetics, but I was still riding the novelty high so I enjoyed the experience. In retrospect, I can see that I was already mistaking enjoyment of the experience as comprehension of the material. Sure, the International Phonetic Alphabet looked a little weird, but I thought I was catching the main gist of it. I was pretty decent at transcription, easily pumping out examples like: /naɪf/=knife. I even vaguely understood why this might be useful in teaching a new language given that the "kn" and silent "e" would probably not translate easily outside of English. Between my comprehension of this part of the lecture and 10/10 on the first homework assignment, I felt pretty good about my performance in those first couple of weeks.

Unfortunately, neither my positive feelings nor performance lasted. Before too long, I was utterly lost. I'm not sure exactly when it happened, but it felt like there was very little warning. It can't be that one day I understood completely and the next day I understood nothing, but it felt exactly like that. The manner of articulation content was the worst; I could not hear the subtle differences between sounds that were made in different parts of the mouth. I also couldn't understand why we would need to be able to explain that /o/ is a mid/back/rounded vowel and /i/ is a high/front/unrounded vowel when teaching English as a foreign language. My question wasn't motivated by the complaints of "why do we have to know this?" or "when are we ever going to use this?" I simply needed to understand the endgame in order to make sense of what we were doing.

I asked my question in class, but rarely got an answer that I understood. The instructor could not have been more patient and kind, so I don't think it was lack of effort on his part. Many of my classmates asked varieties of the same question, but we seldom got clarity on this point. My theory is that the instructor experienced what Wiggins and McTighe (2005) call, the *expert blindspot*. The expert blindspot occurs when something is so obvious to the teacher that they cannot conceptualize the learner's lack of understanding of that point. Driving is the quintessential example of this phenomenon. It's difficult for someone who has been driving for decades to remember that a new driver has to be told to put their foot on the brake, slide the key into the ignition, etc. We tend to start with "back out of the driveway" rather than explaining all these earlier steps that we've been doing so long that they are automatic to us. I later learned from a tri-lingual friend that the reason one needs to understand manner of articulation is that not all languages have the same sounds. This was undoubtedly obvious to our multilingual instructor who probably did make the connection in class, but may not have done so explicitly and repeatedly enough for monolingual students without his linguistics background.

Most of what I did learn during those lost weeks occurred with my friend's daughter, Reshmi, who was also in the class. I'll discuss our collaborative learning process more in the next chapter. We studied for the first test together and shared a sense of foreboding as the test day approached. I was not shocked to have done poorly on it, but the day I received it back was one that will always stick with me. As the instructor placed the test (face down, thankfully) on my desk, I had that feeling I can only describe as the one you get when you feel yourself falling. You're pretty sure you're going down, but a small part of you holds out hope that you can catch yourself in time. You want to hold onto that moment of not knowing what's probably true. So, I waited for a second, then lifted the page, very slightly, like it was too hot to touch. Yep, it was a 33.5/50 all right. I didn't know the exact calculation immediately, but I knew it was bad. My mind launched into a series of self-directives. Put it back down so Reshmi doesn't see. So no one sees. Put it in your bag. Remember to take it out later and hide it so it doesn't fall out.

I looked over at Reshmi, who was scowling at her test. She gave me the thumbs down sign, then threw the test in her bag with an aggravated sigh. It was the end of class and we walked out, complaining and speculating about how the rest of the class did. We both had places to be, but agreed to confer later. We sent each other many texts throughout that day, mostly of the resigned humor variety. I knew our jokes were a distancing mechanism, but it felt good to have a friend in this nonetheless. I wondered how I would have felt if Reshmi had done well on the test. (She later confessed to me over drinks that her terrible grade was only a B). Then I started to wonder how my students felt when they struggled in my classes.

I went back to my office and was truly incapacitated for a couple of hours. I was past the initial shock, but unable to concentrate. I didn't know what to do. What would I tell a student in this situation? I would tell them to make an appointment with me to discuss what they had missed on the exam. This advice that I had always given so freely now seemed wildly brave. Face the instructor? No, thank you. What I wanted to do, of course, was drop the class. I wish I could say that it was courage that kept me from doing so, but it was actually the embarrassment of too many people knowing I was taking this class. Even though I could make an excuse about being too busy, Reshmi would know the truth. I was sure she was classy enough not to announce my failures, but even one person knowing I had quit was enough to give me pause about dropping.

So, I didn't know what to do. I tried to put the 67% aside and focus on other things. That didn't work. After a couple of minutes that turned into hours of trying to discharge the anxiety through online shopping, Facebook, and other useless activities, it occurred to me that I was having a truly new experience. I realized that I was not following any of the advice I gave students in these situations; in fact, I was doing the exact opposite. I was avoiding, distancing, and wasting time rather than dealing with the issue proactively. I now understood, at least in a limited way, why students do seemingly irrational things in response to struggle. I had a glimpse into the process by which denial and shame get a hold of students and cause them to behave in self-defeating ways. If I could lean into this experience, I could gain a better understanding of my own struggling students.

FEAR AND SHAME

My self-defeating behaviors echo those described in *The College Fear Factor*, a qualitative study of how college students experience learning (Cox, 2009). Fear was the central theme in Cox's findings. Fear was such a powerful force that it drove students to avoid tests and difficult assignments, hide from faculty, and live in uncomfortable denial while getting further and further behind in courses. That last point was especially salient because fear tended to have a snowball effect. Relatively low stakes failures that could have been managed with early intervention often spiraled out of control not because the students were incapable of doing the work, but because their fear was so intense that it paralyzed them.

I have found that understanding this phenomenon is key to working effectively with struggling students. In the absence of such an understanding, faculty tend to misdiagnose students as apathetic and/or unintelligent. I can appreciate this tendency, having made this mistake many times myself. Behaviors like silence in class, absence from office hours, and failure to turn in assignments look like lack of motivation and/or intelligence. Yet, I know now that many students exhibiting these behaviors are actually doing so out of the fear that leads to paralysis.

Part of why I can make this claim is that it was clear to me as a student that I was not the only one whose behavior changed after the first test. Some students simply did not come back to the class once we received our first grades, a phenomenon consistent with Cox's (2009) findings about struggling students. Perhaps a clearer understanding of student struggle would better inform the considerable efforts universities devote to retention efforts. More specifically, Cox (2009) noted that the students in her study experienced so much shame as the result of their struggle that nearly all of them would only discuss it with her in the past tense (p. 39). In other words, students who were struggling in the moment were unlikely to be willing to talk about it. The students who would participate in the study did so when they were safely on the other side of the struggle, talking about it as a past problem rather than a current reality.

I admit that this need to succeed before really acknowledging, much less admitting, failure characterized my own experience as well. It took weeks before I summoned the courage to tell my own wife about my first test grade. I didn't tell anyone else about the extent of my struggles in this course until I had passed it. On the surface, this can seem like a fairly benign story of ego, but the ramifications are consequential. It appears that, for some students, their experience of fear and shame is so incapacitating that all they can do is quietly disappear from a class.

While most of the students in my class did not drop it after the first test, they engaged in other distancing behaviors. Two women who sat next to me, for example, diligently took notes and paid attention in class before the first test. In the days that followed, they became mildly disruptive, whispering to each other and ignoring the instructor's ban on devices. Before the first test, it did not appear that these two students even knew each other. The shift in their behavior was significant enough for me to notice, even in a class where I was trying hard to focus on the material.

Before experiencing struggle for myself, I would have interpreted these students' behavior as disrespectful, which maybe it was. But as a struggling student, it made more sense to me. Reshmi and I, too, seemed to want to talk more in class after the first test. My desire to talk was not driven by an active desire to disrespect the professor; it seemed more motivated by the need to connect with another person who also felt lost. Also, I learned what is probably obvious to most students: class is boring when you don't understand what is going on. It's actually hard to refrain from talking or playing on your phone when you're so confused that you can't even formulate the questions that might shed some light on the subject. I managed not to talk or text, but mostly because I felt some solidarity with the instructor as a fellow teacher. In the absence of that identification, I don't know that my behavior would have been any better than my fellow students'.

Even though I had been telling students for years to get help early if they're struggling in class, it turned out to be very difficult to follow that advice. Part of the reason lies in academia's penchant for framing struggle in ways that erase the affective dimension. Despite years of student development research demonstrating the importance of holistic learning, we seem to be moving further in the direction of solutions that focus on students' heads rather than their hearts. There are entire industries dedicated to "early detection" software and other apparatuses designed to promote student success and retention. Higher education leaders spend millions of dollars on these products rather than reducing class sizes and advising loads, which sends a clear message about how they conceptualize the problem. Students largely accept this frame, rarely demanding more personalized attention and instead seeking tips and strategies for getting better grades. In fact, the current generation of traditional age college students is known for its squeamishness about the more emotional dimensions of life, making it even less likely to manage challenging emotions like fear and shame.

"Catching Feelings"

The students in my linguistics class belong to what is called either Generation Z or iGen; I will use the terms interchangeably to refer to this group since there is not yet a consistent name for them. Born between 1995 and 2010, these students are best known for their lack of life without technology, a topic I'll discuss in Chapter 6. They are also known for their high levels of mental health issues, a phenomenon many consider to be related to their dependence on technology and incapacity for feelings and relationships. I have always been skeptical of generational trends, which seem to devolve into crude stereotypes that show up in mean-spirited ways on social media. Yet, I could not help but notice some of the aspects of Generation Z's tendency toward emotional distance coming out in my Linguistics class.

In the many opportunities I had to listen to students' conversations before and after class, I did not hear a single student (other than Reshmi) admit to being upset about their poor grades. Maybe this is not surprising; it requires a certain degree of vulnerability to admit to being upset. When I was a (Generation X) student in the 1990s, my friends and I tended to avoid this vulnerability by expressing anger toward the professor. The students in my Linguistics class, however, didn't even do that.

They mostly said things like, "whatever," "it'll be okay," and "it's fine." This puzzled me until I started to think of their comments in the context of what their generation calls, "catching feelings."

"Catching feelings" is a term iGen uses to describe what they consider to be the problem of developing an emotional attachment to a person with whom one intended to have a casual sexual relationship (Paul, 2013). I've worked on college campuses my entire adult life, including a variety of positions where I was required to live in residence halls. As a result, not much surprises me, but this notion of "catching feelings" did make me sad on behalf of young people. While the term "catching feelings" refers to sexual relationships specifically, the idea extends to Generation Z's discomfort with authentic emotional expression more generally. Students in this age group report feeling pressured to mirror the beautiful, happy, and carefree images that barrage them in their constant social media engagement (Twenge, 2017). Unfortunately, these images often mask loneliness, depression, and a host of other mental health issues as evidenced by the increase in emotional distress reported by this cohort of students (Prince, 2015).

Mental health issues are not new in the college student population, but the pressure to either avoid expressing feelings altogether or share only positive emotions is a relatively new phenomenon. At its best, positive psychology encourages people to refrain from obsessing about problems so that they can harness their assets and leverage them in the service of solutions. This can be an effective strategy in many cases, particularly given our evolutionary tendency to give outsized attention to that which makes us feel threatened (Vaish, Grossmann, & Woodward, 2008). There is something to be said, however, for moderation. Some argue that the pendulum has swung so far toward positivity that people feel judged for expressing anything that isn't cheerful (Ehrenreich, 2009).

What does all of this have to do with learning? Because I feel free to acknowledge my emotional reality, I was able to do some sense making in terms of my own struggling student experience, verbalizing the issue in something like these words: "I felt fear and shame as a result of that first test grade and these emotions were paralyzing for awhile. Once I diagnosed this problem, I could start to find a way out of self-defeating behaviors and do what I needed to do to move on." I attribute part of my ability to get to this point to being a middle aged professor who teaches on the topic of college student mental health. Traditional age college students without this unique background do not typically express their experience in the language just described. More typically, they dis-associate by engaging in the behavior like the women sitting next to me or another student, who took to signing the attendance sheet, then leaving when the instructor's back was turned.

While I did not disassociate openly during class, the pressure to be dispassionate about my experience caused me to hold the class at a distance. It felt a bit like a phobia; there were days I didn't even want to see my textbook because the thought of opening it and feeling lost again seemed so overwhelming. I did not have Generation Z's fear of "catching feelings," but I did experience what Brene Brown calls "excruciating vulnerability," that extreme discomfort of feeling out of control. Brown's (2015) research shows that most people seek to numb vulnerable feelings, often through destructive measures like alcohol abuse. Even when people choose more seemingly benign methods like distraction or avoidance, the numbing proves problematic because it is not selective. In an effort to numb vulnerability, people numb positive emotions as well, eclipsing their ability to feel much of anything. But even if we could selectively numb vulnerability, my sense is that we would still have a problem. Vulnerability can motivate connection; my openness in sharing a struggle with you hopefully creates a sense of safety that you can do so with me. Vulnerability at its best fosters creativity and connection, two conditions I found essential in deeper learning.

Trying not to feel something is ultimately about control and ego. As long as I kept trying to maintain control/ego, I was blocked from getting the help I needed to address the issue. I was stuck in a spiral of avoidance, distraction, numbing, and then feeling even more lost as I got further and further behind. I've seen this cycle many times with doctoral students who have gotten behind in their dissertation work. If they would address the challenge early when it was relatively minor and therefore manageable, they would be in much better shape later. What many of them did, however, was feel shame at that early missed deadline, then avoid dealing with that unpleasant emotion, then distract and numb themselves with Netflix binges, then miss the next deadline. I began to refer to this phenomenon as the "Evil Vortex of Doom," in hopes of defanging it a bit with a funny name. I relentlessly warn my students against the Evil Vortex of Doom, lecturing them on how self-defeating it is. I now add include a Vulnerability 101 lesson in that lecture because it's important to understand where the Evil Vortex of Doom comes from. It's not a rational response to challenge, but it is a natural reaction to vulnerability. Once students know both how it works and the fact that their professor experiences it, too, they are often better about getting help.

EMPATHY

I, too, had to face my fear, shame, and vulnerability to muster the courage it took to do the last thing I wanted to do after receiving my first test grade. I sent the instructor an awkwardly worded email seeking his guidance. Despite my progress in facing my own vulnerability, I included an easy out in this message, suggesting that we might be in an "old dog, new tricks" situation and, if so, I would drop the class if that was his advice. It wasn't. He wrote that I should not drop the class, but instead come to office hours to go over the test. He offered extra credit. He told me not to worry about it.

So, this is how I ended up on the other side of office hours, which was educational in and of itself. Walking into someone else's office or, in this case, graduate student cubicle, and trying to articulate my lack of understanding of the material gave me a new appreciation for what this process is like for students. It was beyond difficult to help someone troubleshoot my issues when I had so little comprehension of them myself. I credit Selikem with getting into the weeds with me and trying to explain what to him was so simple and obvious.

This experience of being truly lost as a student made me a more effective teacher in terms of asking better questions, putting students at ease, and just being willing to wade into their confusion with them. Before seeing office hours from the other side, I think I was nice enough, but I had limited capacity when students showed up totally confused. My impulse was to repeat explanations I had given in class, which I can now see is not all that helpful. If they had understood what I had said in class, they wouldn't be seeking additional help.

That anxiety is often on our end, too, as faculty who love our disciplines and work to communicate them to students. Sometimes we respond defensively to student struggle because it's frustrating when people do not understand us. Some of our complaining about students undoubtedly comes from this frustration of not being understood despite genuine efforts to help. We can unwittingly feel forced to conclude that either the student is unintelligent or we are incapable of doing our jobs well. Neither is an attractive option, so we can find ourselves avoiding students who present problems without clear solutions. I don't think I ever did this intentionally, but I know that I was limited in my approaches before I understood more fully that struggle is often masked by behaviors that look more like lack of effort. I assumed that if students would simply try harder, they would get it. After all, this strategy had worked for me (before I truly struggled in a class, of course).

Because these reactions to failure resemble disrespect, indifference, and/or ignorance, it can be difficult for faculty to empathize with the students exhibiting these behaviors. I know I've been guilty of this lack of empathy myself as a professor. On a personal level, it requires a lot of patience to devote time and energy to struggling students. The problem is that struggling students do sometimes appear to not be trying. I have to be intentional about not investing all of my energy in students I deem to be more gifted and/or disciplined.

These gifted students are attractive to faculty because they speak our language. They make us feel competent and fulfilled because we know what to do with them. We often describe them as the reason we got into teaching in the first place; the opportunity to help successful students reach new heights is extremely satisfying. My goal is not to take anything away from the sincere joy that comes from working with students who share our love for a subject. But we do need to unpack and name this phenomenon in order to address its role in our giving the most attention to the students who need it the least. It's easy to unwittingly write off students who we perceive as unmotivated.

Arnold (2005) asserts that, "The better we understand how students feel and think about their learning experiences, the better able we will be to construct effective pedagogies" (p. 67). This statement embodies the central theme of empathy, which Arnold positions as integral to the learning process. She illuminates how empathy is necessary to avoid oversimplifying complex phenomena. For example, she explains how the fear of psychic contamination kept some of her students from identifying with a bullied character in a story. On the surface, it appeared that the students were simply insensitive, but a more careful analysis allowed her to observe students expressing a situation in which they could not afford to relate too much to the bullied individual for fear of being exposed themselves. It is this kind of nuanced analysis that is needed if we are to find a way through some of the entrenched challenges of limited student learning.

MINDSET AND GRIT

There has been a palpable shift in higher education from emphasizing innate abilities to cultivating discipline and hard work. Beginning with Carol Dweck's work in the mid-1990s, educators have been encouraged to inculcate the idea that it's effort rather than natural talent that makes people successful. Dweck (2008) framed this distinction in the language of fixed vs. growth mindsets. In her research, she found that young people approach challenges with either the goal of proving their own intelligence or mastering a new skill. Those in the former group become discouraged in the face of adversity and tend to give up. Conversely, those in the latter group exhibit a greater tolerance for the failure that must be endured on the way to success and thus achieve greater heights.

Dweck's (2008) research inspired a craze of sorts in the recasting of failure as a positive. "Fail early, fail often" became the mantra in many sectors, including higher education. This reframing of failure has many positives; it creates a language for helping students to develop tolerance for the hardship that inevitably accompanies substantive achievement. There is also a democratizing aspect to this idea that success comes not from innate capacity but from effort. The logical conclusion is that we're not stuck in some sort of biological determinism that cannot be changed, so we just need to foster resilience in our students and they will have the tools they need to overcome challenges.

Grit is the newer buzzword for this suite of tools. Duckworth, Peterson, Matthews, and Kelly (2007) define grit as "perseverance and passion for long-term goals" (p. 1087). They go onto assert:

> Grit entails working strenuously toward challenges, maintaining effort and interest over years despite failure, adversity, and plateaus in progress. The gritty individual approaches achievement as a marathon; his or her advantage is stamina. Whereas disappointment or boredom signals to others that it is time to change trajectory and cut losses, the gritty individual stays the course. (pp. 1087–1088)

Like mindset, grit helped to move the conversation on student achievement forward by shifting the focus from innate (and therefore largely unchangeable) ability to more accessible skills to be learned like positivity, passion, and perseverance.

The problem is that this change mirrors the broader shift from aristocracy to meritocracy. Meritocracy is better than aristocracy in many ways, not the least of which is that one is not required to be born to a certain family to have opportunity in life. But as Guinier (2016) points out, meritocracy fails to deliver the fairness it promises. People are still born into such grossly unequal circumstances that they do not compete on anything close to a level playing field. Furthermore, the illusion the contest is fair abdicates those with privilege from the responsibilities they were forced to acknowledge under aristocracy.

Some scholars are starting to levy the same critique of grit, characterizing it as a newly repackaged version of the same bootstrap mentality that further marginalizes under-resourced students (Golden, 2017). The hyper focus on effort as the cure for all challenges minimizes the role structural inequality plays in students' ability to succeed. The logic is that poor kids would improve their lot if they simply cultivated habits similar to those in the higher classes, strongly implying that the privileged students' culture rather than the privilege itself accounts for their success.

While most critiques of grit focus on how it diminishes structural considerations, another area of concern I see is its minimization of the emotional aspect of struggle. Thomas (as cited in Socol, 2014) offered an evocative example of this phenomenon in the following analogy:

> Children in poverty line up at the starting line with a bear trap on one leg; middle-class children start at the 20-, 30-, and 40-meter marks; and the affluent stand at the 70-, 80-, and 90-meter marks. And while gazing at education as a stratified sprint, "no excuses" reformers shout to the children in poverty: "Run twice as fast! Ignore the bear trap! And if you have real grit, gnaw off your foot, and run twice as fast with one leg!" These "no excuses" advocates turn to the public and shrug. (p. 11)

The grit literature's near obsession with work makes it susceptible to a certain degree of callousness in some peoples' interpretation. The original mindset and grit scholarship emphasized the role of effort as something that ought to be of comfort to students. They could feel less burdened by the outmoded attitude that success is due to inherent talent and focus instead on cultivating good work habits, which presumably anyone can do. At their best, mindset and grit can serve as antidotes to imposter phenomenon because they reframe talent from something that is innate to something that can be acquired.

In retrospect, I can see that the tenets of resilience and grit helped me in challenges where I have the foundational skills I need to accomplish the task and just need to push past the human urge to procrastinate. Writing, for example, is one of those areas where I am beyond college-ready. Dweck and Duckworth's work has helped me to achieve greater productivity in writing by giving me the language to identify my desire to abandon more difficult tasks in favor of the easier items on my "to do" list. For students struggling with this specific problem, the mindset and grit literature can be helpful in naming and addressing the issue.

Hence, I do not seek to minimize the value of mindset and grit; these concepts have helped me enormously both with my own work and in coaching students through the well-known challenges of writer's block. My point is to expose the limits of resilience and grit in cases where students are truly lost. For example, I doubt that grit would do much to help me if I didn't already know the fundamentals of writing. Grit can help me move through the middle and later stages of tough intellectual work, but it doesn't work as a substitute for that foundational knowledge one needs to get started on a task.

The critiques of grit rang true for me in my experience of struggling as a student because working harder was largely ineffective as a strategy. I went to office hours and did the extra credit assignment I was fortunate to receive there. I read the assignments more closely and took better notes on them. I reviewed the lectures the instructor helpfully posted on Blackboard and took notes on those as well. I dropped other things in my life and devoted myself to the study of linguistics. These things made no difference; in fact, I got the same grade on my second test as I did on my first, 33.5/50 or 67%.

MINDFULNESS AND METACOGNITION

The first two test grades I received in Linguistics were transformative for me. Working harder had been the way I re-established control in my life, yet it proved utterly useless in this case. The more I tried to cram into my already full head, the less I seemed to learn. This was true emotionally as well. I was so full of fear, shame, and anxiety about this class that it was nearly impossible to concentrate. I started to realize that trying to be in control all the time might be causing the problem. Perhaps the solution could be found in letting go and emptying my mind. These are counter-intuitive impulses in a culture that places a premium on doing more things in less time.

Like most students, I did not learn much when overwhelmed by shame and anxiety. As mindfulness proponents wisely point out, there is no space in a mind that is already full. Students receive a lot of advice related to time and study management, but these things are of limited utility when you're really struggling. In my own experience, reading the textbook and reviewing notes mattered much less than I would have predicted.

What mattered much more than I would have predicted was being able to slow down. When we're stressed out, our impulse is often to speed up and power through. Sometimes, this strategy works, but only in sprint situations where a last minute push can get us where we want to be in a short time period. In a marathon situation—which is more akin to a 15-week semester—the sprint strategy is unsustainable and can end up being counterproductive. I can see in retrospect how that first test grade lit a fire that stimulated me to obsess unproductively. I felt like I was working because the frenzy was exhausting, but I wasn't actually accomplishing anything. I wasn't really focusing; I was doing the intellectual equivalent of sprinting in circles.

My second 67% test grade turned out to be a blessing in disguise because it was the result of an accidental experiment. After the first 67% test grade, I hypothesized that working harder would yield better results. When I earned the second 67%, I was a little heartbroken at first. But upon mindful reflection, I also saw the emancipatory potential in that second 67% because it was evidence that my old ways weren't all that useful. Failure became the license to try on new ways of being.

By the time I received the second 67% grade, I was journaling about my experience as a student with the idea that I might write about it someday. This act allowed me to practice what the educational literature calls, *metacognition*. At its most literal, *metacognition* means thinking about thinking. Though metacognition can sound esoteric, there is a large and growing body of research demonstrating its importance in the learning process (Zimmerman & Schnuk, 2011).

Metacognition is what empowers people to exercise agency over their own learning. Taking the time to slow down and problem-solve rather than simply cramming in more information proves to be a good investment of time. In my own case, I started asking the multilingual people in my life how they learned a new language. Once I could see how grammar functions as the common ground between languages, some of what I was learning in my first linguistics class started to make sense. I began to see how a person had to develop some capacity to analyze patterns in a speaker's first language to be able to explain the internal logic of the target language. This is probably beyond obvious to my linguistics instructor, but I couldn't really grasp the proverbial trees until I understood a bit about the forest. When I started formulating my own questions, I could read and listen to the material through a frame that made sense to me.

"We Feel, Therefore We Learn"

Once I started to make sense of what I was learning, the class became a lot more meaningful to me. It may seem obvious that meaning matters in education, but attention to the affective realm is a relatively recent phenomenon. Advances in neuropsychology have stimulated interest in the impact of emotions on learning. In their aptly named work, *We Feel, Therefore We Learn: The Relevance of Affective and Social Neuroscience to Education*, Immordino-Yang and Damasio's (2007) explain how the neuropsychology community made a breakthrough in its understanding of the connection between thought and feeling. They discuss how traditional neuropsychology underestimated the role of feelings in rational thought, explaining "Emotions were like a toddler in a china shop, interfering with the orderly rows of stemware on the shelves" (p. 4).

Despite this assumption, researchers noticed that some neurological patients who had suffered damage to the emotional and social functions of the brain also began to make irrational choices. Neuroscientists began to ask questions about why patients whose brains' affective dimension had been compromised would also show signs of diminished cognition. Because these patients had no loss of IQ, researchers expected that their decision-making capacities would remain untouched. Instead, they found that thought and feeling worked more in tandem than previously assumed. Without the insights made possible by emotion, patients engaged in faulty reasoning. As Immordino-Yang and Damasio's (2007) went on to explain, "…emotions are not just messy toddlers in a china shop, running around breaking and obscuring delicate cognitive glassware. Instead, they are more like the shelves underlying the glassware; without them cognition has less support" (p. 5).

In light of these recent revelations, Immordino-Yang and Damasio's (2007) and other scholars building on their work advocate for the concept of emotional thought, a construct that acknowledges the inseparability of thought and feeling. In her later work on this topic,

Immordino-Yang (2015) extended the research with her findings regarding the specific role of positive emotion on the brain.

It is important to distinguish this focus on positive emotion and its connection to learning from the excesses of positive psychology. As discussed earlier in this chapter in the context of the grit literature, some scholars have begun to point out the ways in which positive psychology can be taken too far. David (2017), for example, warns that forcing positivity can make us feel insecure about our ability to handle negative emotions. Constantly trying to control ourselves so that we feel only the positive creates its own set of anxieties. Perhaps equally problematically, obsession over trying to be happy all the time creates an outsized focus on the self, which tends to inhibit the kind of mindfulness required for deeper learning.

I found David's assertion to be true in my own experience of the negative feelings that came with struggle. When I tried to deny, repress, or otherwise distance myself from them, I felt even more stressed out about my ability to succeed in the class. When I practiced self-compassion, my experience resonated with the students Bain (2015) profiled in his book, *What Successful College Students Do*:

> People who discover how to comfort themselves generally suffer less anxiety. They take greater responsibility for their own lives. They are more peaceful, their minds are more open, and they are less likely to make those social comparisons that breed prejudice. College students who score high in self-compassion suffer less anxiety and depression, develop greater satisfaction with themselves and their lives, find more joy in just learning for its own sake, and avoid the trap of worshipping high grades. (p. 174)

Perhaps paradoxically, the distinction both David and Bain point out is that fulfilled people are capable of losing themselves to some extent. Rather than focusing so hard on the individual self and what makes it feel happy, fulfillment comes from losing the self in something bigger.

Smith (2017) picks up this theme of something bigger in her research, which identified both happiness and the self as entities for which excessive focus in one's life could diminish satisfaction. She draws attention to recent studies showing that an outsized focus on happiness could lead down a path away from meaning. Meaninglessness, in turn, was positively correlated with depression and suicidality (Oishi & Diener, 2014). Pursuing a "giver" sense of meaning rather than a "taker" form of happiness, conversely, pushed people toward lives of "connecting and contributing to something beyond the self" (Smith, 2017, p. 15).

Smith goes onto connect this sense of connection to something bigger as the force that helps us persevere: "When we devote ourselves to difficult but worthwhile tasks—whether that means tending a rose or pursuing a noble purpose—our lives feel more significant" (p. 35). We're able to lose ourselves in the service of what we have to give, thus allowing us to recapture that energy we expend on ego and use it to develop more creativity and motivation.

PURPOSE, REFLECTION, AND DEEPER LEARNING

I experienced a shift that echoes Smith's (2017) point about the importance of being able to let go of one's ego in the service of something bigger. When I realized my default ways were no longer effective, I became more self-conscious initially. I worried about what my low grades said about my intelligence and that preoccupation stressed me out for awhile. But failure also opened the door to experimentation, forcing me to examine the gaps in my understanding at a deeper level. Through that reflection process, I got back in touch with what had stimulated my desire to earn the TEFL certificate in the first place. I had wanted to help people.

Helping people is often a noble goal, but it is also fraught with potential complications. Many scholars draw attention to the ways in which paternalistic and colonial impulses can undermine peoples' ability to be truly helpful (Bringle, 2015). Privileged people imposing their religion, culture, and/or economic system on developing countries provide the most obvious examples, but more subtle forms of paternalistic help occur as well. Without thoughtful reflection and critical analysis about the nature of how one thinks they might help, it's easy to act from an ill-informed mental model about the target of one's help.

I can see now that this gap in my own understanding was a big part of why I struggled in that first linguistics class. As a monolingual speaker of the world's most privileged language, I really had no idea about how people learn a new language. I took my foreign language requirements in high school and college, but was never expected to function in Spanish. I was taught by bilingual teachers whose knowledge of both English and Spanish made them very effective in framing the target language with an understanding of how students' native language would inform their learning.

When I finally accessed my memories of these classes, I began to under-stand that I would be teaching students about whose native languages I was totally ignorant. The reason I needed to understand the basics of linguistics was to have the tools I needed to understand where my future students were coming from.

I cringe at this revelation now, realizing I had been so blind to the importance of non-English languages that I was operating from mis-guided assumptions about what it would mean to teach English as a foreign language. I so utterly failed to grasp the essence of what I was trying to help people do that I couldn't understand the material. I had to engage in what Grisold, Kaiser, and Hafner (2017) called *unlearn-ing* the old to be able to receive the new content. This is why work-ing harder had been ineffective; it doesn't matter how fast you're going if you're headed in the wrong direction. Deeper learning often requires slowing down so that a person can see the defaults from which they've been operating. We go through life so quickly that we develop templates that function as shortcuts for getting things done. When they work, defaults and templates serve us well. They fail, however, when things change and a new paradigm is required to operate effectively. Without critical and ongoing examination, defaults and templates stifle the cre-ativity we need to imagine other ways of doing things. Once I realized that this had happened to me in the context of my first linguistics class, I started to develop the new ways of thinking I needed to get unstuck.

Reconnecting with my purpose for being in the class allowed me to engage in the kind of reflection I needed to learn more deeply. By no means did I grasp the material perfectly, but I did go from 67% grades to earning an A in the class. I learned the content well enough to improve my test scores, but more importantly, I eventually understood at a more fundamental level why I was learning it. Critical reflection played an important role in that process of unlearning my biased default assump-tions, but connection with other people was probably even more crucial in my movement from confusion to clarity.

CONCLUSION

Before I experienced life as a struggling student, I was a good advice giver. I thought I was being compassionate, pointing out over and over again that effort matters more than innate talent when it comes to achieving one's goals. I invoked mindset and grit almost religiously, promising students that hard work would always pay off. When struggling was theoretical to me, these seemed like good ideas. I don't think they're bad ideas now, but I do see that they're insufficient. Once I actually experienced struggle for myself, I could understand how frustrating it must be for students to be told to try harder when they're too lost to even know what to try. Trying harder works when you know what it is you need to do and just need the motivation to do it. Effort is also effective when a student is just a little bit lost and needs to develop the tolerance for ambiguity it takes to work through confusion and get to a place of clarity. My experience taught me that deeper levels of struggle require more complex interventions. One of these solutions came in the form of community, the focus of the next chapter.

REFERENCES

Arnold, R. (2005). *Empathic intelligence: Teaching, learning, relating*. Sydney, NSW: UNSW Press.

Bain, K. (2015). *What the best college students do*. Cambridge, MA: President and Fellows of Harvard College.

Bringle, R. G. (2015). *Crossing boundaries: Tension and transformation in international service-learning*. Sterling, VA: Stylus Publishing LLC.

Brown, B. (2015). *Daring greatly: How the courage to be vulnerable transforms the way we live, love, parent, and lead*. New York, NY: Penguin Books.

Cox, R. D. (2009). *The college fear factor*. Cambridge, MA: Harvard University Press.

David, S. (2017). *Emotional agility: Get unstuck, embrace change, and thrive in work and life*. New York, NY: Avery.

Duckworth, A. L., Peterson, C., Matthews, M. D., & Kelly, D. R. (2007). Grit: Perseverance and passion for long-term goals. *Journal of Personality and Social Psychology, 92*(6), 1087–1101.

Dweck, C. S. (2008). *Mindset: The new psychology of success*. New York, NY: Random House.

Ehrenreich, B. (2009). *Bright-sided: How the relentless promotion of positive thinking has undermined America*. New York, NY: Metropolitan Books.

Golden, N. (2017). There's still that window that's open: The problem with "grit". *Urban Education, 52*(3), 343–369.

Grisold, T., Kaiser, A., & Hafner, J. (2017, January). Unlearning before creating new knowledge: A cognitive process. In *Proceedings of the 50th Hawaii International Conference on System Sciences (HICSS-50)*. Maui: IEEE Computer Society Press.

Guinier, L. (2016). *The tyranny of the meritocracy: Democratizing higher education in America*. Boston, MA: Beacon Press.

Immordino-Yang, M. H. (2015). *Emotions, learning, and the brain: Exploring the educational implications of affective neuroscience*. The Norton Series on the Social Neuroscience of Education. New York, NY: W.W. Norton.

Immordino-Yang, M. H., & Damasio, A. (2007). We feel, therefore we learn: The relevance of affective and social neuroscience to education. *Mind, Brain, and Education, 1*(1), 3–10.

Oishi, S., & Diener, E. (2014). Residents of poor nations have a greater sense of meaning in life than residents of wealthy nations. *Psychological Science, 25*(2), 422–430.

Paul, E. (2013). Beer goggles, catching feelings, and the walk of shame: The myths and realities of the hookup experience. In D. Kirkpatrick, S. Duck, & M. Foley (Eds.), *Relating difficulty: The process of constructing and managing difficult interaction* (pp. 141–160). New York, NY: Routledge.

Prince, J. (2015). University student counseling and mental health in the United States: Trends and challenges. *Mental Health & Prevention, 3*(1–2), 5–10.

Smith, E. E. (2017). *The power of meaning: Crafting a life that matters*. New York, NY: Random House.

Socol, I. D. (2014). Taking a closer look at the grit narratives. *Knowledge Quest, 43*(1), 8–12.

Twenge, J. M. (2017). *IGen: Why today's super-connected kids are growing up less rebellious, more tolerant, less happy—and completely unprepared for adulthood—and what that means for the rest of us*. New York, NY: Simon & Schuster.

Vaish, A., Grossmann, T., & Woodward, A. (2008). Not all emotions are created equal: The negativity bias in social-emotional development. *Psychological Bulletin, 134*(3), 383–403.

Wiggins, G., & McTighe, J. (2005). *Understanding by design*. Alexandria, VA: Association for Supervision and Curriculum Development.

Zimmerman, B., & Schnuk, D. (2011). *Handbook of self-regulation of learning and performance*. New York, NY: Routledge.

CHAPTER 4

Success Through Connection

Abstract This chapter highlights the people and practices that helped me to move through academic struggle. Although the concepts described here were not new to me, I had somewhat of a shallow appreciation for them before my experience as a struggling student. For example, I valued collaborative learning, but understood it as somewhat peripheral to the educational enterprise. I was surprised at the central role being able to connect with another human being played in my ability to persevere through struggle. In this chapter, I identify how moving past my bias toward individualism into a more community-oriented understanding of learning allowed me to get unstuck. My goal in this chapter is to stimulate readers' ideas about how they might use collaboration, experiential learning, and community engagement as ways to provide transformative educational experiences for their own students.

Keywords Collaboration · Experiential learning · Deep learning · Unlearning · Community engagement

In the last chapter, I described the depths of my struggle in my first linguistics class. I experienced the darkest moments of that struggle alone. In retrospect, words like "darkest" and "alienation" feel too dramatic. I was just taking some classes, after all, not fighting in a war or battling a life threatening illness. This realization is a good one; perspective allows us to avoid becoming too self-indulgent.

© The Author(s) 2019
L. M. Harrison, *Teaching Struggling Students*,
https://doi.org/10.1007/978-3-030-13012-1_4

Yet, the psychological world reminds us repeatedly that we humans often fail to think rationally. We feel the fight/flight/freeze emergency response even when there is not a clear and present danger. We engage in self-destructive rumination, scanning the horizon for perceived threats to our worthiness, especially in situations we deem to be competitive. These are parts of the human condition that can lead to underperformance if left unattended to. Fortunately, mindfulness can serve as a powerful intervention in mitigating this faulty thinking, even in terms of interrupting the fight/flight/freeze response (Kabat-Zinn et al., 1998). The slack/time wealth I discussed in Chapter 2 is largely what allowed me to interrupt these patterns.

The process of moving from frenetic wheel spinning to relaxed contemplation was largely a spiritual one for me. I eventually learned to freak out less so that I could pay attention more. I started to experience what Zajonc (2006) described in terms of attention as a form of love. What was once arduous and overwhelming became more like the pleasurable satisfaction that comes with solving a difficult puzzle.

I experienced a sense of what scholars have variously called *surrender* (Dewey, 1939), *transcendence* (Emmons, 1999), and being *rapt* (Gallagher, 2010). Instead of frantically trying to gain control of the situation, I gave myself over to it in a sense. I allowed myself to get lost in the material without worrying so much about the consequences. I abandoned cramming and let my own questions and curiosities guide my engagement with the course content.

Most importantly, I followed Langer's (2016) advice to pay less attention to one's performance and more attention to the work itself. In *The Power of Mindful Learning*, she presents compelling research suggesting that both skill and effort-based measures of performance limit our ability to thrive. She asserts that traditional education makes people too self-conscious, which detracts from our ability to focus on the work itself. She contrasts school with games, where we tend to be more experimental rather than evaluative:

> We make a move, it works or it doesn't. We make a face or curse and move on. When it doesn't work, we try something new...Instead of rating our performance, I think it would serve us better to train mindful attention to the particulars of the game. (p. xx)

By letting go of my own ego, I began the process of getting unstuck and thus began to discover new approaches to learning material that was not intuitive to me. This spiritual journey through struggle was instrumental in helping me to succeed in the TEFL program. But even this progress only got me so far. I hit a wall in my ability to persevere on my own. I eventually moved past fear, but I didn't move toward courage until I developed meaningful connections with other people.

Having a Friend in the Class

I intentionally named this section with words that might elicit a question like "Isn't that a little juvenile?" in the reader's mind. I may have responded the same way before becoming a student myself. For some reason, it's easy to minimize the role of peers in higher education, the assumption being that college students should have outgrown the need to sit by their friends in class. I will admit without shame that it mattered a lot to experience this class with a friend by my side. Though empathy has many merits as discussed in the previous chapter, it also has limits. As Zahavi (2010) argues astutely, we project our own experience onto other people. Despite our best intentions, we overestimate our mind's capacity to transcend real differences in experience (Warren & Hotchkins, 2015). This doesn't mean that we shouldn't try to understand one another, but it does mean that there is something uniquely helpful about being able to talk to another person who is experiencing the same phenomenon.

It was simple good luck that created this possibility for me. Reshmi's presence in that first linguistics class shaped my experience as a student far more than I ever would have anticipated. What began as a funny coincidence turned out to be one of the most significant aspects of my student experience. Reshmi is the daughter of one of my friends; I was at a party at her parents' house one evening a few weeks before the start of the semester when the topic of my enrollment in the TEFL certificate program came up. Reshmi mentioned that she was taking the same class and her mother joked that it would be funny if Reshmi and I were in the same section of the class. We checked our respective course schedules that night on her laptop and learned that this was indeed the case.

Reshmi joined the class late, having been delayed in returning to school after the winter break. I remember feeling happy on the third day of class, January 13, 2017, when she walked into the room and sat down next to me. She greeted me warmly, then launched into an analysis of the news, including Trump's statements about banning migrants from Muslim-majority nations. Both her presence and the discussion topic made me feel less out of place in the student section of the classroom.

I had been enjoying the class before Reshmi's arrival, but it had been awkward at times sitting in a class of 18–22 year olds, especially on the first day of icebreakers. Reshmi's presence made the class feel more like a public lecture I was attending with a friend.

We carried on an animated conversation about our fears for humanity under a Trump presidency. We seemed loud in a classroom where there were other people, but none of whom were talking. I wondered if any of our fellow students were Trump supporters; it seemed statistically impossible that none of them were. I scanned the room and noticed my mind quickly defaulting to stereotypes in the Trump supporter detection game I had begun to play. I ruled out the woman sitting next to Reshmi who was wearing some sort of animal ear costume headband and therefore struck me an alternative type. I had already decided on the first day that the thin, attractive, polite young man sitting to my front left of was probably a member of the LGBT community, so he was not a likely Trump supporter. I zeroed in on two sorority-looking women to my immediate left and began speculating on their views. They definitely looked like my mental model of Trump's young female fans. They did not seem disturbed by Reshmi and my conversation, though, so I couldn't tell. I kind of wanted to ask them, but I didn't because I noticed that Reshmi and I were almost always the only people talking before class.

THE CLASSROOM AS A NON-COMMUNITY

Many of our mornings in class began this way with Reshmi and me as the only two people talking in a room of 25 students. I often wondered if anyone was offended by our discussions, at first out of anxiety, but then just out of curiosity. I found it odd that I sat with the same people three days a week for 15 weeks without learning most of their names. I had someone with whom I could both pass the time before class started and troubleshoot the more challenging aspects of the course. I wondered whether the other students had these kinds of connections and, if not, how they felt about that. There were times I wanted to ask the other students about their experience, but there seemed to be an unwritten rule about not imposing on one another's space. It was a little like the feeling one has on public transportation where the other people are not necessarily hostile, but it would be strange to start talking to them. It occurred to me that Reshmi and I were the outliers with our frequent talking.

Our outlier status was so noticeable to me that I checked in with Reshmi's mother about it to make sure that she didn't feel pressured to talk just to be polite. Her mother assured me that Reshmi likes middle-aged people, which seemed consistent with her voluntary presence at gatherings I'd attended with her mom and our other faculty friends. I was so curious about the other students' silence in our class that I asked my own students about it, noting that they were anything but quiet before, after, and sometimes during class. Their consensus was that "the younger generation" was even more connected to their devices and less inclined to engage in person than older people had accused them of being. I teach graduate students, many of whom are not much older than the undergraduate population, but they, too, noticed a distinction.

During the first few weeks of the class, this observation was simply interesting to me. I didn't think it was necessarily important to the academic enterprise itself. Then, I began noticing that the lack of talking extended to the class itself. It may not matter whether students interact before and after class, but the silence during class seemed to reflect a lack of participation and engagement. I remember feeling badly for the instructor on many occasions, wondering how I would respond if my students stared at me blankly when I asked questions. There was one exception, though, a student who sat in the front row and answered nearly all of the instructor's questions.

The one eager student is such a common phenomenon that this person is parodied in both media and real life. Stanford students refer to this person as "IHum boy/girl," meaning that one person who always has their hand raised in the Introductory to the Humanities course required of all first-year students. Reshmi and I named the IHum boy in our class "Professor Guy," an irony that was not lost on me. Nathan (2006) was so intrigued by this phenomenon of the one eager student and other students' reactions to this person that she conducted an experiment in her own class. As an anthropologist, she created a class on the role witchcraft plays in some cultures. She developed an exercise in which she asked the students to speculate (anonymously) on who the witch in their class might be. Even in her large lecture classes, there has been remarkable consistency in students identifying the "IHum boy/girl" in her class as the witch. When Nathan became a student herself as part of her own anthropological research, she saw more clearly how there is an unwritten rule among students that too much perceived alignment with the professor is looked down upon.

One would think that this would be untrue for Nathan as a student since she is also a professor, but she wrote of feeling that same sense of discomfort in being perceived as engaging too much in her classes (p. 91). I was surprised by my own hesitation to talk in class, especially given that I preach participation to my own students. I had always assumed that students didn't talk in class either because they cared too little about the content or cared too much about looking cool. Neither of these reasons explained my own reticence yet I found it very uncomfortable to talk in class, even when I knew the answer and felt empathy for the instructor. Nathan posits that students confuse equality with invisibility, believing that speaking up creates the perception that they are aligning too closely with the authority figure in the room (p. 91). This makes sense to me, but I also wonder if there is a certain vulnerability that comes with showing too much engagement or excitement. My own students talk, but they are graduate students who seem to have more permission to be "nerdy" or "geeked out" about school.

Whatever the cause, classrooms can be sterile places without intentional cultivation of shared experience. Nathan recounted a conversation that illustrates the pervasiveness of students' silence:

> One particularly sensitive community college professor told me, "I never use professional jargon in my classes, because if my students didn't understand what I was saying, no one in the class would ever ask me." As a student, I realized that he was right. "What does that mean?" is, incredibly, just not the kind of question that an American college student would ask. (p. 92)

This story resonated with my experience as a student during what our instructor attempted to create as interactive lectures. Fortunately, he was perceptive about this issue and built assignments into the class. These opportunities for collaborative problem-solving were where I observed the most participation in the class. Selikem moved from the front of the class to the student section where he toggled between groups to answer questions. This seemed to break down the student/instructor wall and move the class toward more collective engagement. The only times I interacted with anyone in the class other than Reshmi were during these in-class assignments where we were required to do so.

The word, "requirement" sometimes has a negative connotation, especially among people like me who favor less hierarchical classroom dynamics. But for students whose default is invisibility for whatever reason, a requirement can sometimes feel more like an invitation or even permission than an authoritarian demand. One of my own students explained this to me recently. I had her in three consecutive classes and noted that her writing was markedly better in our last class together. I had assumed that her progress had come naturally through practice, but fortunately had the idea to ask her to share her own thinking about how she had improved so much. She looked at me a little sheepishly, then said, "Well, you made us go to office hours in the last class, so that helped me understand what I was doing wrong." I was genuinely surprised; I had a good rapport with this student and would have thought that she would have come to office hours voluntarily in my other classes. When I expressed that perception with her, she responded, "I know in my head that going to office hours is not a sign of weakness, but that's how it's perceived. Or people think that only great students go and have intellectual conversations with the professor." I asked her if I should start requiring office hours and she agreed that I should, adding "Then it would just be a normal thing to do."

I've shared that story with numerous students since then and they have all validated her perception that office hours are for outlier students on either end of the performance spectrum. One person added that some cultures have norms that discourage office hours attendance due to a perception that it is impolite to take up professors' time. Requiring office hours was a simple fix to these barriers. I realize in retrospect that I probably would have never thought to ask my own struggling students about their experiences had I not struggled recently myself. The experience of struggling has made me ask better questions of my own students and really listen to the answers. Teaching is too often reduced to either technique or personal qualities, both of which of course play a role in effectiveness. Overemphasizing those factors places too much focus on the teacher when often what is needed is actually in the student. More specifically, it can be easy to overlook the role of what students and teachers alike learn in the context of community.

CONNECTION AND LEARNING

Before I had experienced life as a struggling student, I underestimated the importance connection plays in one's ability to get unstuck academically. As a person with a background in counseling, I understood the significant role relationships play in helping people to move through personal challenges. I also appreciated the connection between the emotional and intellectual theoretically, but not as thoroughly as I did once I actually had to access that connection to solve real problems.

This connection manifested in several ways in my relationship with Reshmi. There was the emotional support level, which we both accessed on more than one occasion, particularly the day we received our first tests back. This experience is consistent with a growing body of scholarship documenting the importance of connection in students' ability to navigate the feelings of disappointment, frustration, and embarrassment that often accompany academic failure (Museus, Yi, & Saelua, 2017; Rayle & Chung, 2007; Strayhorn, 2012). Having a shared experience allowed us both to surface, express, and ultimately manage emotions that, left untended, can diminish the self-efficacy needed to recover and face the next challenge.

"I'm so grateful you're in this class." "I would be flunking this class without you." "I'm glad someone in my life can relate to this experience." These are sentences Reshmi and I said to one another at least once a week through our semester together. The positive feedings generated by our relationship empowered us to engage in more expansive sensemaking than either of us would likely have achieved on our own. I had been aware of this research, but failed to fully appreciate it until I had experienced the power of collaborative learning myself.

In addition to the emotional support integral to learning, the ability to work with Reshmi helped enormously in mastering the course content. Barkley, Major, and Cross (2014) define this experience as collaborative learning, "two or more students laboring together and sharing the workload equitably as they progress toward intended learning outcomes" (p. 4). I don't know that I had experienced collaborative learning before this class. I had been in classes where professors required group work, but I don't recall actually problem-solving with a peer before Reshmi and I began tackling our Linguistic studies together. My performance as a "good student" had been decidedly solo, a reality of which I had not been consciously aware until circumstances dictated the acquisition of new ways of being. This was an epiphany of sorts, realizing that my only options weren't success or failure entirely on my own.

THINKING TOGETHER

I'm not sure of the exact timeframe during which Reshmi and I began consistently studying together, but I do recall our shared determination that Morphology would not best us the way Phonetics and Phonology had.

According to the syllabus, we started our Morphology unit on February 22nd, which is likely accurate since we followed the syllabus fairly religiously in this class. During the previous five weeks of the class, Reshmi and I did text each other with homework questions and studied together from time to time, but mid-February was when the class became more of a joint project for us.

We drew a lot of word tree diagrams over pizza at my house on those cold, February evenings. These meetings contrasted with the isolating fear, shame, and anxiety I described in the last chapter. Just being with another person got me out of my head and tempered my crippling self-consciousness. Working with Reshmi specifically helped me to move from paralyzing ego-centrism to the energy that comes from being a part of something bigger than oneself. I was now into a project with a person I respected and enjoyed; not wanting to let her down turned out to be a big motivator. I knew I would be sunk if Reshmi gave up and dropped the class. The last thing I wanted was to do that to her.

My experience of studying with Reshmi reflected Hanson, Trolian, Paulsen, and Pascarella's (2016) summary of their research findings on the benefits of collaborative learning:

> Compared to competitive or individualistic efforts, working with peers is associated with positive learning outcomes. Students who work with peers are more willing to take on difficult tasks; are able to retain more knowledge; and have increased use of critical thinking and creative thinking skills, increased ability to transfer knowledge, more positive attitudes toward tasks, increased time on task, better social and communication skills, and increased self-esteem. (p. 193)

Cognitive scientists, Sloman and Fernbach (2017) explain that these benefits are possible in collaborative learning because people are able to engage in a cognitive division of labor. As the world becomes increasingly complex, they argue, this capacity for collective intellectual work will become even more important because individuals simply cannot hold all the information they need at all times. They debunk the metaphor of the brain as a computer, pointing out that the brain is only designed to hold what it needs at the moment and is very efficient at filtering out what it deems to be extraneous. Hence, the adaptive mind is the one that can work harmoniously with others in what cognitive scientists call *intentionality*, that is, shared attention toward mutual goals. Both our ability to act intentionally and the positive emotions we experience as a result of it are part of what distinguishes humans from other animals (p. 14).

This intellectual and emotional synergy defined my experience of working with Reshmi. Filtering the material through our own frameworks and understandings allowed us to build on our strengths and troubleshoot our growth areas. In a sense, we borrowed each other's brains for trying out ideas, diagnosing faulty reasoning, and sharing "aha" moments in comprehending concepts. In *Powers of Two: How Relationships Drive Creativity*, Joshua Wolf Shenk (2014) highlights the historical overemphasis on individual achievement, arguing that most truly creative breakthroughs involve more than a single individual. He goes further, making the less obvious point that groups of 3 or more also have drawbacks in their ability to promote creativity, positing that "pairs naturally arouse engagement, even intensity. In a larger group, an individual may lie low, phone it in. But nobody can hide in a pair" (p. xxii).

Shenk's (2014) words resonated as I reflected back on my years as a traditional age student who definitely took advantage of the hiding opportunities inherent in large classes. Even in classes where I felt both competent and interested, my attitude toward collective assignments was similar to the negative responses often expressed by my current students. In the absence of intentional integration into a larger vision, collaboration can slip into the dreaded group work scenario. An assignment that seems easier to complete on one's own becomes a hassle as students try to coordinate schedules, manage work styles, and deal with the seemingly inevitable problems of the slacker members. I myself have tried to sell group work as a great opportunity to learn important skills like cooperation, but students often either resist or resign themselves to the situation as another hoop to jump through.

My experience working with Reshmi helped me to see the benefits of pairs, which contain both the benefits of another perspective without the inconvenience of too many logistical and personality issues. Perhaps as importantly, part of what worked for Reshmi and me is that we chose to engage in collaborative work with one another. There is a different level of investment when students are empowered to exercise some agency over their learning. I now offer my students the option of working with another person in most assignments and have seen the "powers of two" produce higher quality, more novel work in my own students.

Still, there are circumstances in which deeper learning necessitates a broader collective experience. This is where Parks' (2011) notion of the tribe is instructive. In her seminal work on how college students develop purpose and meaning, Parks posits the tribe as "a place of dependable connection, where we have a keen sense of the familiar: ways of knowing and being that anchor us in a secure sense of belonging and social cohesion" (p. 116). The tribe's corollary, tribalism, is under increasing attack for its role in the divisive politics eroding our sense of community and collective ability to accomplish important work. At its best, the tribe represents the opposite of this destructiveness, instead empowering individuals to be their best selves by allowing them to draw on the strength of the group. Though I did not experience a tribe in my first few classes, I found it in the final course.

Experiential Learning

While I've talked primarily about my experience in my first linguistics class, it makes sense to introduce my capstone class at this point. The middle three classes occurred online; I'll address those experiences in the next chapter. The capstone class fits in this chapter because it embodied the best of the themes discussed here in terms of community and connection. In addition, it provided the sole experiential learning experience in the program. Keeton and Tate (as cited in Kolb, 2014) define experiential learning as:

> ...learning in which the learner is directly in touch with the realities being studied. It is contrasted with the learner who only reads about, hears about, talks about, or writes about these realities but never comes into contact with them as part of the learning process. (p. xviii)

Experiential learning opportunities allow concepts to move from ethereal to visceral so students can connect with them more readily. This is essential to the intellectual process of grasping the material.

The practicum experience put me in touch with the realities of linguistics and was therefore the most salient learning experience I had in the program. Once concepts became more tangible, they made a whole lot more sense. The reflection and action components of my practicum experience were instrumental in understanding some of the material that had eluded me in the conventional classroom.

For example, one of the assignments in the practicum class was an observation of an instructor teaching in the Ohio Program of Intensive

English (OPIE). One of my former students happened to be teaching in this program, so I chose his class to attend. Many of the concepts I failed to understand in my first linguistics class suddenly became clear to me when seeing them applied in real life both in his class and in the one I would eventually teach as part of the practicum. For example, one thing I learned by observing my former student's class is the purpose of the International Phonetic Alphabet. I had vaguely understood why the International Phonetic Alphabet might be useful, but did not actually comprehend it until I saw my former student use it to explain a sound the student had in her own language, but which does not exist in English. This may seem like a small point, but it made a huge difference in my learning process to be able to move past an abstraction into more concrete application.

Similarly, I learned how being able to explain voiced and voiceless consonants mattered in showing subtle distinctions like "butter" versus "budder" when my students correctly pointed out the challenge in hearing the difference in American English. My practicum experience exemplified the best of experiential learning both academically and personally which, as it turns out, cannot really be distinguished. As Newcomb and Wilson (1964) asserted many years ago, learning beyond the surface requires an "overlap" of the intellectual and spiritual. We divide academic experiences by disciplines and semesters and maybe it is necessary to do so to have some kind of structure. The reality is that learning at its best is not really contained by these constraints.

For example, I did not understand the utility of the concept of minimal pairs from my first linguistics class until I had graduated from the TEFL program. A couple of months after the program, I had volunteered to serve as a Global Conversation Partner and the person with whom I was paired had done some teaching abroad. He showed me how it is useful to be able to isolate the sound responsible for the difference between words as in "cat" versus "cot." He explained that this is a particularly useful technique for articulating sounds that do not have counterparts across languages. Up until this point, the minimal pair was just something I had to memorize and recall on a test, not an actual technique with application in terms of my own real-life goals.

It wasn't reticence that caused me not to grasp minimal pairs in my first class; I was not simply complaining in the childish "when are we ever going to use this" sense. But not knowing when we were ever going to use this had a real impact on my comprehension. Our instinct as faculty is to start with theory first, then show how it applies in practice. The TEFL program I completed was set up in this way with highly conceptual courses first, then practical ones later. The problem with that design is that students often can't understand a concept until they have at least some idea of how it might be applied. Students' questions along this line sometimes appear as complaints ("why do we have to know this?") or vocationalism ("I don't see how that's relevant in real life").

My practicum experience helped me to reconnect with the frustration behind those complaints. Students simply get bored and unmotivated when it's not clear how something matters in real life. Relatedly, much of conventional classroom learning requires studying on one's own and demonstrating mastery via tests and papers. While these activities have their place, there has been a heightened appreciation for more interactive forms of learning. Examples include first-year seminars, learning communities, internships, capstone courses, and community-based learning, all of which have been identified as "high impact practices" according to Kuh's (2008) extensive research on student success. The idea is that these kinds of educational activities challenge students to engage more actively with the material as empowered participants rather than passive recipients. Ultimately, the point is to move past the surface learning that often accompanies more passive forms of education into the kinds of deeper learning that stick with students far beyond the completion of a course.

Deep Learning

There is always a challenge in reconstructing a story from memory, even with extensive notes and other artifacts. I felt this challenge often in the course of writing this book, but almost never when writing about the practicum experience. I remember the practicum experience vividly because it engaged my mind and spirit.

Chickering (2006) offers an important distinction between *training* and *education*. He argues that the goal of training is to "take a collection of diverse personas and make them more alike" by giving them a common skillset (p. 130). He takes care to point out that there is value in training; one does not want to be treated by an untrained physician, flown by an untrained pilot, etc. But he posits education as existentially different from training, calling out its Latin root, "to lead out or draw forth" (p. 130). The educational process does not make students more alike, rather it builds on each individual's goals and talents. My practicum class exemplified this definition of education; I felt both lead out and drawn forth throughout the eight weeks I spent teaching English as a Foreign Language.

Before our practicum class began, Gaby, the professor set up a meeting to go over the logistics. She provided pizza. She smiled warmly. The class had many moving parts and it wasn't entirely clear how it would work. As someone who likes things to be planned, this would normally have worried me. But Gaby was so enthusiastic and relational that I believed in her.

We would be teaching in the English for All program, an outreach initiative provided for those on campus or in the local community seeking to improve their English. I was assigned to the beginner class, a small group of four students. I felt fairly confident as I walked into class that first night. Although the topic was different, I had been teaching for many years and felt secure in my ability to transfer my knowledge of teaching generally to this new subject.

That turned out to be a false sense of security. I am embarrassed to admit this now, but I somehow managed to be blindsided by my students' lack of ability to understand me. I don't know how I could have thought I was going to be able to explain the course in a language that was almost completely foreign to them. In my limited experience as a student in foreign language courses, I had the benefit of teachers who were bilingual and classmates who shared my first language. The teacher could explain the instructions in English, then move into Spanish, toggling effectively between the two. I could offer my students no such benefit.

So, I spent much of that first night smiling dopily and muddling through. The two Turkish students brought their English-speaking daughter to class so she did a lot of translating for them while I spent more time with the other two students. I normally teach 3- and 7-hour classes, both of which feel fairly fast-paced to me. The hour I spent in my first English for All class felt much longer, but not because it was unpleasant. It was simply exhausting to try to explain things across a large language barrier and I felt like I was scrambling a lot of the time.

In my scrambling on that first night and some subsequent class sessions, I found myself tempted to hide. I came across one of my own former professor's description of a similar experience, which I quote at length because it captures one of the most honest expressions of a common phenomenon for teachers at all levels:

> I had been asked to teach courses in which I had little preparation, and I was struggling to stay one lesson ahead of my students. One morning at the blackboard, I noticed that I was attempting to disguise my handwriting to cover my uncertainty about the spelling of a few words I needed to write. I also realized that I had developed the art of giving ambiguous answers, delving into another subject in which I had some expertise, or telling distracting stories whenever I was unsure of the answer to their questions. What was I really trying to achieve, I wondered? What value did all my dissembling have for my students? How could I possibly believe that I was gaining their respect? And if they did indeed hold me in some respect, what false model were they respecting? Was I really telling them to cheat, to be insincere, to hide their limitations rather than confront them. (Ada, 2007, p. 106)

Ada's (2007) words resonate with an experience educators discuss privately, but rarely admit publicly for many reasons, not the least of which has to be the constant negative bombardment by those who seek to discredit public education from kindergarten through graduate school. Another reason it is difficult to admit much less openly share such experiences is the genuine discomfort that tends to accompany putting one's self out there and not having it go well. Yet, academics need support to do this very thing in order to keep stretching ourselves. If we succumb to our anxieties, we'll keep playing it safe which often leads to less than engaging learning experiences for our students.

That sense of scrambling I experienced the first night of the English for All class is what Freire (1970) called the "shock" of deeper learning. He posited that learning beyond the surface level required something of a jolt to shake our consciousness and thus allow us to see in new ways outside of old paradigms. As my English for All class progressed, I experienced this shock on several occasions. In the beginning, the disorientation made me feel a little vulnerable because I was embarrassed at not being able to function in the classroom space I normally inhabited with competence. But I eventually experienced a high degree of pleasure in the disorientation as I started to realize it as a source of creativity.

Part of what makes it possible to admit vulnerability is simply a sounding board. Because Gaby is such an engaged and encouraging professor, I found myself wanting to talk to her about my growth areas.

As discussed previously, observation is one of the most effective methods for improving teaching yet faculty often don't take advantage of it out of fear of being deemed ineffective. I had a similar squeamishness about being observed as part of the tenure process, but welcomed Gaby's presence in my practicum class teaching. She not only showed up, but took detailed notes and presented them in a way that allowed me to push myself without fear of condemnation. Her skill and sensitivity as a teacher promoted the kind of deep learning that challenges students to tolerate the heightened emotion that accompanies trying difficult tasks without getting caught up in feelings of fraudulence. Her willingness to self-disclose her own learning process also modeled the importance of facing one's fears with authenticity and courage.

One of the other practices that promotes deep learning is reflection (Nelson Laird, Seifert, Pascarella, Mayhew, & Blaich, 2014). I'm a little sheepish to admit this given that I require reflection when I teach, but being required to submit reflections annoyed me at first. I saw it as yet another thing to remember in a fairly dizzying set of requirements for the practicum. Not only were students expected to teach several times a week, we had to do observations, create lesson plans, and put together a final portfolio with several labor-intensive components. All of this had to be achieved during a compressed summer schedule, so the thought of doing reflections just seemed like another hoop to jump through.

Once I actually started writing the reflections, however, I experienced the value of slowing down and examining the experiences I was having more intentionally. I'm certain I would have missed the deeper insights I gained if I had been allowed to rush from task to task without stopping to construct a thoughtful analysis of these experiences. Being required to reflect on my work opened the door to more complex thinking, which allowed me to break through the confirmation bias discussed in Chapter 2. Instead of simply replicating what I already knew, I ventured into more interesting and imaginative terrain by allowing myself to feel less sure and more ambiguous. This sense of disorientation characterizes the phenomenon of unlearning, a process some consider to be a first step in transformative educational experiences.

UNLEARNING AND TRANSFORMATION

There are many contested ideas about the purpose of education, but its role in transforming students is one around which there is much consensus. It is generally accepted that students are not supposed to leave educational institutions the same way they came in. In other words, they are supposed to change in some fundamental way. People dispute the nature of that change, some arguing the purpose of education as the acquisition of employable skills while others see character building and/ or critical thinking as more important. *How* students should change is up for debate, but the idea that they should change is generally accepted.

MacDonald (2002) posits unlearning as a key component of the kind of change that occurs in transformative education. The idea is that one cannot truly consider new knowledge or ways of being without critically examining the old. Unlearning requires discomfort, so much so that MacDonald suggests that there is a grieving element to the process as one begins to let go of the tried and true to wander cognitively into less familiar terrain. While often fruitful in the end, unlearning necessitates a period in which students feel unsure and off balance. Part of effective teaching is helping students to negotiate the ambiguity without resolving it prematurely, thereby impeding the unlearning process.

During my practicum, this experience of disequilibrium forced me not to default into old ways of being and doing as a teacher. Having to slow down, listen for gaps in understanding, and adjust in real time allowed me to access the more patient and flexible parts of myself. And, as it turned out, those are the parts of myself I like best. I like the version of Laura who doesn't react with annoyance or anger when an activity fails, who can laugh at the situation and adapt.

I got the opportunity to do this when I attempted to recreate the famous marshmallow challenge in class one night (see https://www.ted. com/talks/tom_wujec_build_a_tower should you want to try this). The basic idea is to use teambuilding skills to erect the largest tower possible using uncooked spaghetti and marshmallows. There were too many moving parts for this activity to go well, but we ended up having an interesting talk about whether marshmallows conformed to Islamic dietary rules. Students came to different interpretations, one Muslim student choosing to snack on the marshmallows and another refraining. The existential nature of marshmallows turned out to be a surprisingly interesting discussion theme among the students.

Unlearning also allowed me to access a deeper level of openness to the brilliance of other people. A small, but powerful example of this occurred when I realized how right the professor was to make us submit detailed lesson plans before class. Like most college faculty, I had never taken a class teaching. This strange feature of university life has been discussed extensively, but the tradition of college faculty receiving little to no pedagogical instruction persists. As a result, I had never been required to make a lesson plan and it felt strange to do so. I didn't necessarily mind doing it, but it seemed counter-intuitive to the kind of loosely structured, student-centered teaching I try to practice. The detail required of these lesson plans felt foreign and unnecessary to me at first, but I did them diligently in order to not lose the points that would be deducted if I had failed to submit them.

By unlearning my default class preparation strategy, I quickly learned that lesson plans are a good thing if you're not teaching graduate students in your own field, largely in your shared first language. I cannot even imagine how many mistakes the lesson plans helped me to preempt by requiring me to think through an activity before doing it. I know I constructed more thoughtful learning experiences that incorporated talking, listening, reading, and writing than I would have without having to plan so thoroughly. The intense planning freed me up to be more spontaneous and present in class because I didn't have to think about what was coming next. I don't plan for my current classes in as much detail as I did in the English for All program, but the experience did make me rethink my own teaching in ways that I think improved it overall.

Service Learning and Community Engagement

Unlearning is frequently a part of service learning or community engagement, both terms used in the higher education literature to characterize the kind of class my practicum was designed to be. Service learning and community engagement are terms used to describe courses designed to be mutually beneficial for students and whatever community they serve in a particular class. There has been a recent shift toward the term community engagement as some view service as a word that connotes a paternalistic sensibility. Both terms occur frequently in the literature, so I will use them interchangeably here.

Community engagement enjoys widespread popularity as an approach to both student learning and service to those outside the university setting. Based on extensive research on its effectiveness, community engagement is considered to be a high impact practice as discussed previously in this chapter (Kuh, 2008). Community engagement is not without its critics, however. Perhaps the most clearly stated and frequently cited objection comes from Illich's (1968) aptly named piece, "To Hell with Good Intentions." In this address at the Conference on InterAmerican Student Projects, Illich advised:

If you have any sense of responsibility at all, stay with your riots here at home. Work for the coming elections: You will know what you are doing, why you are doing it, and how to communicate with those to whom you speak. And you will know when you fail. If you insist on working with the poor, if this is your vocation, then at least work among the poor who can tell you to go to hell. It is incredibly unfair of you to impose yourself on a village where you are so linguistically deaf and dumb that you don't even understand what you are doing, or what people think of you. And it is profoundly damaging to yourselves when you define something that you want to do as "good," a "sacrifice" and "help". (para 34)

Though I had read this piece before, re-reading that last in the context of my own goals with the TEFL program admittedly stung. There are differences between my work that of Illich's (1968) addressees; I was not engaged in any sort of service tourism, nor were my students economically disenfranchised. But I was trying to do "good" and "help," even if I would argue that my motivations were not the paternalistic versions of these goals. In fact, I felt responsible as a white, middle class American whose country had just elected a xenophobic despot to at least try to be of service to those most targeted by the President's hateful rhetoric. 'Besides, what is the alternative?,' I silently argued with Illich, 'Those with privilege simply being selfish and not even attempting to do anything positive?'

I'm still duking it out with Illich in my head. I think I'm right on the idea that people have at least try to be of service, though the point is well-taken that much of this activity could be more thoughtful and truly collaborative. But he did get me thinking more critically about my specific project of teaching English, a language that dominates the world as the result of the very worst impulses of colonialism. Was my service learning experience an endorsement of this ideology, even tangentially? Did I think critically enough about my initial desire to be of service after what I perceived to be a disastrous election result? Would it have been more responsible to invest my time, energy, and money on efforts directed toward political change rather than service? Is it possible that I actually acted against my own goals by taking space in classes, conversations, and service efforts where people with more expertise may have been more productive?

Service learning at its best raises these kinds of questions in the minds and hearts of those who participate in it. I have only thought this deeply in a handful of other classes I've taken in my life, all of which were over a decade ago. My experience in the practicum resonates with some

elements of what Mitchell (2008) distinguishes as critical service learning. Although the critical scholarship that helped me to formulate the
aforementioned questions actually occurred in classes I took before
the practicum, they provided a framework for helping me to interrogate
the structural issues I might have missed in my service learning experience.

This transformative learning is often used to counter Illich's and others' critiques about the limited impact service learning has in amelio-
rating social ills. The logic is that while service learning may not always
achieve significant outcomes for the community, it remains valuable due
to its potential for causing students to think more critically about power
and privilege. This was certainly true for me and the idea has widespread
appeal in higher education. Despite the attractiveness of this notion,
Butin (2006) surfaces a problematic aspect of this thinking:

> Service-learning thus finds itself positioned as attempting to deliver a very
> specific and highly political notion of the truth under the guise of neu-
> tral pedagogy. Its overarching stage theory of moving individuals and insti-
> tutions from charity-based perspectives to justice-oriented ones, in fact,
> maps directly onto our folk theories of what constitutes Republican and
> Democratic political positions: Republicans believe in individual respon-
> sibility and charity while Democrats focus on institutional structures and
> social justice. (p. 486)

While these distinctions work fine for my political sensibilities, Butin is
right to point out that educational institutions have serve a wide ideological spectrum. In the same piece, he references conservative writer, David
Horowtiz's, advice to students to use the left's words against them. For
example, "hostile learning environment" and "underrepresented" can be
applied to evangelical Christian and/or Republican students with skillful
framing. So the issues are complicated, to say the least. My point here
isn't simply to highlight hot topics in service learning and community
engagement, but to show how participating in it allowed me to think
more in more complex ways about things I thought were done deals
in my life. For example, I have not changed my political affiliation, but
Butin's argument did make me think more critically about being relevant
to students across the ideological spectrum. I don't know that there is a
neutral pedagogy, but engaging authentically and openly with the real
issues rather than conflating my own views with uncontested goodness
seems like an important first step.

CONCLUSION

The practicum experience's relevance in real life helped me to connect to the conventional classroom material. Together, my first and last classes in the TEFL program comprised a deep learning experience that transcends my time in the program. I continue to work with global conversation partners and international students in much more informed ways than I would have without the knowledge gained in both classes. In addition to expanding my mind, these opportunities to learn deeply in the context of community were spiritually fulfilling as well. They deepened my commitment to both my original goal to be of service and the goals I began to form along the way in terms of more creative and imaginative teaching. The practicum class in particular empowered me to access a better version of myself in the best sense of education's Latin root, "to call forth."

REFERENCES

Ada, A. F. (2007). A lifetime of learning to teach. *Journal of Latinos and Education, 6*(2), 103–118.

Barkley, E., Major, C., & Cross, K. (2014). *Collaborative learning techniques: A handbook for college faculty*. San Francisco, CA: Jossey-Bass.

Butin, D. (2006). The limits of service-learning in higher education. *The Review of Higher Education, 29*(4), 473–498.

Chickering, A. (2006). Curricular content and powerful pedagogy. In A. Chickering, J. Dalton, & L. Stamm (Eds.), *Encouraging authenticity & spirituality in higher education* (pp. 113–144). San Francisco, CA: Jossey Bass.

Dewey, J. (1939). *Art as experience*. New York, NY: Capricorn Books.

Emmons, R. A. (1999). *The psychology of ultimate concerns*. New York, NY: Guilford Press.

Freire, P. (1970). *Pedagogy of the oppressed*. New York, NY: Continuum.

Gallagher, M. (2010). *Rapt and the focused life*. New York, NY: Penguin Books.

Hanson, J., Trolian, T., Paulsen, M., & Pascarella, E. (2016). Evaluating the influence of peer learning on psychological well-being. *Teaching in Higher Education, 21*(2), 191–206.

Illich, I. (1968). *Toe hell with good intentions. In Conference on Inter-American Student Projects*. Cuernavaca, Mexico.

Kabat-Zinn, J., Wheeler, E., Light, T., Skillings, A., Scharf, M. J., Cropley, T. G., … Bernhard, J. D. (1998). Influence of a mindfulness meditation-based stress reduction intervention on rates of skin clearing in patients with moderate to severe psoriasis undergoing photo therapy (UVB) and photochemotherapy (PUVA). *Psychosomatic Medicine, 60*(5), 625–632.

Kolb, D. A. (2014). *Experiential learning: Experience as the source of learning and development.* Upper Saddle River, NJ: Pearson Education.

Kuh, G. D. (2008). *High-impact educational practices: A brief overview.* Association of American Colleges and Universities. Retrieved from http://www.aacu.org/leap/hip.

Langer, E. (2016). *The power of mindful learning.* Boston, MA: Da Capo Press.

Macdonald, G. (2002). Transformative unlearning: Safety, discernment and communities of learning. *Nursing Inquiry, 9*(3), 170–178.

Mitchell, T. D. (2008). Traditional vs. critical service-learning: Engaging the literature to differentiate two models. *Michigan Journal of Community Service Learning, 14*(2), 50–65.

Museus, S. D., Yi, V., & Saelua, N. (2017). The impact of culturally engaging campus environments on sense of belonging. *The Review of Higher Education, 40*(2), 187–215.

Nathan, R. (2006). *My freshman year: What a professor learned by becoming a student.* New York, NY: Penguin Books.

Nelson Laird, T. F., Seifert, T. A., Pascarella, E. T., Mayhew, M. J., & Blaich, C. F. (2014). Deeply affecting first-year students' thinking: Deep approaches to learning and three dimensions of cognitive development. *The Journal of Higher Education, 85*(3), 402–432.

Newcomb, T., & Wilson, E. E. (Eds.). (1964). *College peer groups: Problems and prospects for research.* Hawthorne, NY: Aldine de Gruyter.

Parks, S. D. (2011). *Big questions, worthy dreams.* San Francisco, CA: Jossey Bass.

Rayle, A. D., & Chung, K. Y. (2007). Revisiting first-year college students' mattering: Social support, academic stress, and the mattering experience. *Journal of College Student Retention: Research, Theory & Practice, 9*(1), 21–37.

Shenk, J. (2014). *Powers of two: How relationships drive creativity.* New York, NY: Houghton Mifflin.

Sloman, S., & Fernbach, P. (2017). *The knowledge illusion: Why we never think alone.* New York, NY: Penguin Books.

Strayhorn, T. L. (2012). *College students' sense of belonging: A key to educational success for all students.* New York, NY: Routledge.

Warren, C. A., & Hotchkins, B. K. (2015). Teacher education and the enduring significance of "false empathy". *The Urban Review, 47*(2), 266–292.

Zahavi, D. (2010). Empathy, embodiment and interpersonal understanding: From Lipps to Schutz. *Inquiry, 53*(3), 285–306.

Zajonc, A. (2006). Love and knowledge: Recovering the heart of learning through contemplation. *Teachers College Record, 108*(9), 1742–1754.

CHAPTER 5

Floundering Online

Abstract This chapter focuses on the role technology played in both my in-person and online classes. Touted for its ability to offer widespread access to higher education on the cheap, the digital university is on the rise. I experienced some benefits of online resources, such as being able to find supplemental videos that aided in my understanding of some of the more technical aspects of the subject matter. Being able to slow the videos down and watch them repeatedly is a benefit not afforded by the traditional lecture. More often than not, however, technology hindered my ability to learn by depersonalizing the educational experience and impeding deeper thinking through constant distraction. The point of this chapter is to provide an account of one person's experience so that readers might leverage technology's potential benefits and guard against its negative effects.

Keywords Online education · Distraction · Technology fundamentalism · Dehumanization · Mental health

I closed the last chapter by discussing the profound impact connection with others had on my experience as a struggling student. Working with Reshmi one-on-one and learning in the context of my practicum community deepened my understanding of both the course material and my connection to it. Both of my in-person classes in the TEFL program stretched me in ways I had not anticipated, surfacing and challenging assumptions about the world and myself I didn't even know I had. These transformative experiences were often humbling because one assumption I held without realizing it is that educated, middle aged people should not need some of the lessons I learned. I had considered paternalism and colonialism before, but generally and theoretically. I had not dug deeply into my own complicity in these phenomena, having always thought about them as distant concepts rather than realities that could touch my life in any meaningful way.

I now realize the inaccuracy of my assumption that life-altering learning is for the young. Maybe it was always true, but I see more clearly the importance of continuous education given the lack of stability and continuity that characterizes contemporary existence. Mary Catherine Bateson articulated this truth eloquently and prophetically many years ago, "Unless teachers can hold up a model of lifelong learning and adaptation, graduates are likely to find themselves trapped into obsolescence as the world changes around them" (1989, p. 14). It's possible that we need transformative educational experiences even more as we age; I know I had more to "unlearn" in my 40s than in my 20s. Lifelong learning is vital in our complex and ever-changing world. Having to slow down and reflect on what I was learning helped me to challenge the limitations of my understanding.

The reflection component of my practicum stimulated deeper learning by giving me time to consider the dynamic interplay between my understanding of the world and the experience I was having. This process of slowing down is essential for the unlearning required of deeper learning. Having to submit journals after every class made me pay more attention both to the experience and my responses to it. For example, it was difficult when teaching in the English for All program to present material that both met the students' needs in terms of simple language and honored the complexity of the content. I noticed this in a unit on holidays. Talking about the 4th of July led into interesting terrain about the founding of the United States. I wanted to both present multiple perspectives on the topic and stay true to the goal of the class to provide beginner level English instruction. It was humbling not being able to express myself easily, which was a lesson in itself. This was an educationally rich moment in the class that may have gone by unnoticed if I had not been prompted to recall it for the reflection assignment.

One of the great things about reflection is that it causes us to slow down and pay attention in a world where we often mindlessly jump between things without ever having the full experience of them. Philosopher Simone Weil wrote, "In the intellectual order, the virtue of humility is nothing more nor nothing less than the power of attention" (1952, p. 116). Her words resonate as I reflect on the power of attention that made my process of humility possible. In both my in-person and online classes, however, screens often lured me away from practicing this particular virtue of humble concentration. I was surprised by this problem as someone who does not particularly love being online. When I examined my experience in the context of the literature on human and computer interaction, I learned quickly that actual enjoyment has very little to do with our decreasing attention spans in the context of the digital world. Without intentional countermeasures, many of us experience technology as a phenomenon closer to addiction than fun, especially when trying to accomplish intellectually complicated tasks.

In this chapter, I discuss the role technology played in both my in-person and online classes. Technology in education is something of a wedge issue as views are often simplistically cheerful or harshly critical. My goal is not to rehash the well-worn arguments, rather I seek to communicate the insights I gained from being a student in the digital age. My hope is that these insights will inform readers' understanding of technology from a student perspective so that they can avoid the pitfalls and capitalize on the positive uses.

Screens and Community

Everyday I entered my first class, nearly all the students around me silently scrolled on their phones. They usually put their devices away once class began, but I noticed more phones throughout class once we were past the first few weeks of the semester. Students generally honored the instructor's technology ban toward the beginning of the course, but gradually began to break it as the semester wore on. I wondered if there was some sort of self-soothing going on. The material only got harder as the semester progressed, so it seems unlikely that boredom was the culprit. Yet, even if students had continued to honor the technology ban during class, their preoccupation with their phones before class would have still caused them to miss the opportunity to connect with the people around them. Instead of interacting with what Powers (2010) calls "the crowd" of the internet, the students could have been talking with each other, thus forming relationships with people who were having the same experience as them and more likely to be in a position to offer both academic and moral support.

The crowd Powers describes inhibits both our ability to be alone and in community with the specific people around us. When we interact constantly with a digital crowd, we lose both the depth of our own inner life and the intimacy that comes with fewer, but more committed relationships. In terms of our inner lives, Powers explains "The more connected a society gets, the easier it is to become a creature of that connectedness. One's inner life grows increasingly contingent, defined by what others say and do" (p. 110). My own students frequently validate this claim, complaining of the Fear of Missing Out (FOMO) they feel when comparing their lives to others on social media. This experience does not seem to be limited to the young as older people disclose feeling inadequate when other people post wedding, baby, nice house, and expensive vacation photos. Being a student requires some ability to be alone with one's thoughts, an activity that seems to be fraught with anxiety when constantly weighed against "the crowd."

As importantly, being a successful student means interacting with the other people experiencing the class. In contrast to the crowd of the Internet, these are specific people relating in real time. It's not enough to throw out a post to a general audience and "like" other posts whenever it's convenient. The kind of communication required of students and faculty in classrooms involves a level of precision that can only happen with the immediacy and rapport characteristic of live conversation. Reshmi and I could help each other intellectually and emotionally because we bore witness to one another's experiences in the class. Communal experiences create the powerful connections rooted in shared purpose. They are the balm to the alienation and isolation that too frequently plague our frenzied contemporary existence.

BEING A STUDENT AS A DIGITAL CREATURE

I opened Chapter 3 with a description of what it was like to get my first 67% grade. My first reaction was not to review my mistakes and figure out how to do better on the next test. Instead, I turned to Facebook, a coping strategy that is apparently becoming more common as our brains seek technological fixes to anxiety. As Gazzaley and Rosen (2016) explain in *The Distracted Mind,* our brains toggle constantly between potential sources of both information and solace. Our brains evolved to forage for food, rechecking places we found nutrients in the past and may do so again. While we now seek mental and emotional treats instead of nutritional ones, our neural wiring operates similarly in the digital world as it would in the physical one.

When I opened my Facebook page that day, I was not consciously looking for those emotional treats. In fact, I would have been reticent to proactively seek comfort because I was unwilling to confess my poor grade. But the reflex was motivated by anxiety reduction, so I engaged in the unproductive activity of mindless scrolling rather than facing the grade problem bravely. Even if I had been looking for emotional support, electronic sources have been shown to be far less effective than in-person ones (Seltzer, Prososki, Ziegler, & Pollack, 2012). Either studying or confiding in a friend would have been better uses of my time than staring mindlessly at social media. In fact, researchers have found a negative correlation between Facebook specifically and students' academic performance (Rosen, Carrier, & Cheever, 2013). Hence, my choice was not even neutral, but actively harmful to the goal of academic improvement.

This finding about Facebook did not surprise me because I saw its deleterious effects on my own academic performance as a student now compared with 20 years ago. I don't even particularly like Facebook, but I find myself turning to it when I'm overwhelmed either intellectually or emotionally. During the course of the TEFL program, I wasted a lot of time toggling between Facebook and my work. It took me awhile to gain awareness of social media's role in my academic struggle because I didn't think to look for it. So much of the discourse on social media focuses on the young, which probably played a role in my inability to see it in connection to myself. Yet, when I analyze my notes, it's clear to me that being a student in the digital age definitely made a difference between my experience now and my experience 20 years ago.

I have a healthy respect for technology, gratefully writing this book in a program that allows me to type, store, and search text far more easily than if I had to do so in a notebook or on a typewriter. There were aspects of my linguistics course that were enhanced by technology, such as the Blackboard site on which our instructor posted lectures. I also benefited greatly from the educational videos I found online. Yet, it was monumentally harder to concentrate this time around as a student and that seemed to be the significant downside of technology.

Comedienne Michele Wolf jokes about our culture's curious obsession with "having it all." This expression is usually applied to women who want to have both a career and family, but Wolf uses a buffet as an analogy to show the downside of having it all. Much as one would feel sick and overwhelmed if they had it all at a buffet, too much stimulation can have the same effect. Wolf makes this point in reference to not wanting the full-time jobs of both career and family, but it works in the context of knowledge as well. Much as we don't want to "have it all" at the buffet table, we don't really want all of the information there is on a topic. In order for the material to be useful, it has to be curated and structured in a way that makes sense. Otherwise, we're mindlessly sampling without gaining the true intellectual benefit that comes from engaging more intentionally.

I found myself trying to "have it all" many times in the course of my TEFL program. Although I can't remember my young adult college days with perfect accuracy, I know I focused with greater ease then than I do now. In *The Shallows: What the Internet Is Doing to Our Brains*, Nicholas Carr shares a similar experience of once being able to read books and long articles with rapt attention and now struggling to focus. Like him, I initially assumed that I had lost cognitive capacity due to age. As has been well documented in the neuroscience literature, the more likely culprit is the digital impact. As Carr (2011) explains:

> ...media aren't just channels of information. They supply the stuff of thought, but they also shape the process of thought. And what the Net seems to be doing is chipping away at my capacity for concentration and contemplation. Whether I'm online or not, my mind now expects to take in information the way the Net distributes it: in a swiftly moving stream of particles. (pp. 6–7)

Given the widespread and frequently discussed nature of this concern, it would seem that there would be more hesitance about adding to young peoples' screen time in the form of online education. The obvious counter-argument here is that educationally enriching materials are different from social media, video games, and other digital time wasters. Yet, the McLuhan's (1964) famous quote, "The message is the medium" should at least come into the discussion here. Even if the content is genuinely educational, the medium is not neutral.

As Pinker (2014) documents, digital educational tools have modest outcomes at best. Despite the popularity of the idea of "gamification," changing the delivery does alter the material in a fundamental way. Pinker points out that adults tend to intuit this for themselves, yet settle for "edutainment" for their children: "Though adults love to watch TV and play video games, conflating entertainment with learning is not a mistake most adults make for themselves" (p. 160). Anyone who has spent time with a screaming toddler or bored teenager can guess why parents might want to believe in gamification and edutainment. A better approach would be to acknowledge that there are times when electronic distraction is useful, such as during a long flight. The problem lies with a lack of honesty about the true costs and benefits of digital absorption, especially in the context of education.

Creative Disassociation

I find it difficult to describe my online class experiences because they basically consisted of reading articles, watching videos, writing discussion board posts, and completing assignments. The articles and videos were edifying; I learned a great deal about language acquisition and even felt awe in response to some of the material to which I was exposed. I remember a short, but compelling, article called *How Language Shapes Thought* (Boroditsky, 2011) which made me think about mental models in new and interesting ways. I was fascinated by the idea that Aboriginal children have a remarkable sense of direction because their language uses absolute cardinal directions (north, south) rather than spatial terms (left, right). I vaguely remember studying the Sapir–Whorf hypothesis many years ago, but was excited to be reintroduced to it thought Boroditsky's (2011) work which details how more recent research supports the idea that language influences cognitive processes. The article contained other findings with interesting implications, such as the role gender in language plays in children's acquisition of gender identity.

Similarly, the material in my other online course was often interesting and stimulating. I recently rewatched a video about ethics in English language learning that I recall being particularly interesting. I remember feeling a little sheepish the first time I watched it, having not really considered some of the issues presented in the module. For example, one case centered around the idea of teaching English in a culture where the indigenous language was being wiped out. Another case raised the issue of teaching in a situation where only the elite males of the group would have access to the English classes. Another dealt with an issue similar to the one I had experienced on the 4th of July in terms of discussing complicated issues with limited language proficiency. Another case featured a situation where a person was hired to teach English as part of an outsourcing initiative that would result in the loss of US jobs. This kind of material would have been ripe for the kinds of deeper learning described in Chapter 4 if the accompanying discussion and reflection exercises had been a part of it in any meaningful way.

It was a little surreal to read and watch intellectually edifying material in my online courses and have no one with whom to share it. Both classes had required discussion board posts, but I quickly learned this platform may be the least likely forum for engaging in an actual discussion about the readings. As is typical in online classes, students were expected to post reflections on the texts, presumably to demonstrate having read them. There were penalties both for not meeting word counts and due dates, but it did not appear that the content itself mattered based on the shallowness of most posts (including my own). The only guidelines for the posts were word count, due dates, and politeness. While these are not bad things to consider, they seemed like thin criteria. Critical thought, creativity, and other more substantive qualities were omissions I noticed in retrospect.

Writing and responding to posts was so boring that I eventually made a little game of it, timing my ability to crank out 100 words tangentially related to whatever reading I was required to review that week. I often completed the post before reading the article, just to get the assignment out of the way and ensure not incurring point deductions for late work. This approach struck me as odd from a person taking the class solely for the intrinsic reward of learning. I wasn't just checking requirements off boxes in order to graduate yet, I quickly became very instrumental in my thinking about this class. This strategy echoes what Shahjahan, Wagner, and Wane (2009) call *creative disassociation*:

> ...so must students disengage from their spiritual ways of understanding and knowing the world, as this epistemological framework is not broadly accepted within academia. This results in epistemological dissonance. In fact I would argue that a creative dissociation is a skill developed by many

students, to allow them to survive the academic experience and continue on to complete their degree. (p. 65)

I don't fault my online professors for penalizing late work; I understand the practical necessity of accountability mechanisms. I don't even fault them for the mind-numbing discussion board requirement, a standard feature in online classes conducted on our university's digital platform. In fact, I don't fault them at all because their courses were better than many of their online counterparts in that they offered substantive feedback on assignments.

The creative disassociation results from something bigger than these two courses; it's a product of de-personalized, systematized learning. In all fairness, creative disassociation is by no means limited to online learning; I engaged in some forms of creative disassociation in both my in-person and online classes. The difference is that it was a rare occurrence in my in-person classes. Even when the material was prohibitively difficult and/or boring, I still felt connected to those professors and even fellow students to some extent. These relationships sustained me through challenges and added to the fulfillment I felt during high points in those classes.

The spiritual component to which Shahjahan et al. (2009) refer warrants some elaboration as a concept fairly newly accepted in pedagogical discourse. I use it here not so much in a religious sense, but as a way to try to capture how fragmented and random the online courses felt to me. Unlike the in-person classes that generally engaged my mind and heart, the online material never became a part of me. I mostly read and regurgitated the content without being changed by it. Despite the uninspiring nature of this kind of learning, there has been a trend toward advocating for more of it. Those who argue that universities ought to shift away from their traditional purpose to inculcate critical thinking and instead focus on job training frame education as a neutral enterprise where employable skills are transferred from one brain to another. Ostensibly, the actual goal is not for education to be boring and alienating, rather the focus is on objective knowledge stripped of nuance and controversy and given to students who will become effective workers. Scholars have long argued against treating students as cogs in the wheel of corporate machines on ethical grounds (for example, Giroux, 2015), a position with which I agree. But I also take issue with this approach on educational grounds, arguing that very little deep learning takes place when students are not engaged holistically.

TECHNOLOGY FUNDAMENTALISM

Between 2012 and 2015, online enrollments grew by 11% while campus enrollments declined by 3.2% (Dimeo, 2017). While proponents tout the purported educational benefits, the real motivation appears to be financial. Some believe that online education is the answer to education's financial woes, the idea being that learning can be automated. As I have written elsewhere (Harrison & Mather, 2015), this almost always turns out to be a fantasy as the cost of creating and maintaining these courses tends to exceed projections. Because students are people and not robots, they have needs that prove impervious to automation. Anyone who has encountered a technical difficulty and tried to use a "help" menu can imagine at least roughly why this is. Generic, one size fits all answers seem logical in theory, but almost always fail in practice. Humans need specific, personalized help.

Online education does have some positives when driven by thoughtful design rather than the dream of education on the cheap. One benefit I discovered and wrote about (Harrison, in press) is that there are classes where the online environment allows students to work at their own pace. I teach a scholarly writing class that works well online because struggling students can watch the lectures multiple times without worrying about slowing down the rest of the class. I can offer differentiated instruction based on each student's skill level, helping the more advanced students to move on to new challenges while spending more time troubleshooting with less advanced students. Because my online classes are reasonably sized, I can provide the kind of thorough, individualized feedback students need to learn at a deeper level.

The online classes I took as part of the TEFL program had some of these benefits, especially in terms of feedback. As both a producer and consumer of digital course content, I see some positives and therefore do not intend to critique the whole enterprise in a sweeping fashion. What I find more problematic is the largely uncritical acceptance of online education as the answer to both economic and pedagogical challenges in higher education. This reckless cheerfulness extends to technology more generally as panacea. David Noble anticipated this problem prophetically, observing as far back as the 1970s that, "The imperatives of the automatic market, processional specialization, and rationalized management, coupled with the corporate monopolization of technological intelligence, have contributed to the appearance of technology as an autonomous force in history" (Noble, 1977, p. xxvi).

In other words, Noble exposed the myth of technology as neutral. The "common sense" idea of our own time is something along the lines of: "Technology is neither good nor bad, it all depends how you use it." Foer (2017) exposes the fallacy of this belief, arguing:

> Algorithms fuel a sense of omnipotence, the condescending belief that our behavior can be altered, without our even being aware of the hand guiding a superior direction. There has always been a danger of the engineering mindset, as it moves beyond its roots in building inanimate stuff and begins to design a more perfect social world. We are just screws and rivets in its grand design. (p. 77)

We can see this problem playing out in the capacities we're losing. Stories of young people not being able to maintain eye contact or use the phone confidently now proliferate, but Noble (1977) predicted the problem many years ago. He asserted that "undue emphasis upon the development of technology at the expense of other, equally important activities of human society has resulted in the atrophy of many human capacities and an overwhelming preoccupation with, and obeisance to, the myth of the machine" (Noble, 1977, p. xxi).

I felt that atrophy of ability between my time as a student in the early 1990s and now. Despite advances in maturity and motivation, I experienced some diminished capacity as the result of the costs of being a student in the online world this time around. We extol the many benefits of technology without taking stock of the true costs. One of those costs is the toll technology takes on opportunities for holistic education that engages both heart and mind. While "dehumanization" seems like a strong word, it does express the lack of human connection I noticed in my experience as an online student.

DEHUMANIZATION

The connection I felt in my in-person classes contrasted with the isolation I experienced in my online classes. While technology can be exciting for its utility in gathering large quantities of information, the downside is a sense of alienation an individual can feel when culling through that material.

A big part of the cost is actually what is extolled as the benefit; namely, the templating of course content. The idea that material can be systematized appeals to some because it seems efficient. In my state (Ohio), legislators have been moving toward the goal of standardizing classes. For example, English 101 would be the same at Ohio University as it is at Kent State. This looks like a good plan because employers could presumably know what to expect from graduates of all public higher education institutions in the state of Ohio. Additionally, transferring credits between universities would be easier.

For these reasons, systematizing education makes sense except that it leaves out the most important variable: students. If you think of students as "butts in seats" and "units of enrollment" (both common terms among the more business-driven elements in universities), then the aforementioned plan is nothing short of genius. If you think of students as human beings with all the attending variation in college readiness, emotional maturity, hopes, dreams, confidence, mental health/illness, and so forth, then you realize pretty quickly that any communication with them defies a template.

I knew this truth as a teacher, but learned it again as a student in the TEFL program, particularly in my online classes where my own knowledge and values never informed what was taught. I saw a great contrast in my first in-person class where the instructor was stuck with a template, but deviated from it based on what the students in front of him asked in a given moment. He changed course in real time based on what the students needed. I remember one day when he brought in his own language research to explain how the abstract material we were learning was used in real life. This shift from one-way lecture to multidirectional conversation helped to both clarify the material and inculcate a sense of community in the class. While some of the content in my online courses was genuinely interesting, I never felt engaged as a person whose thoughts, feelings, and values had anything to do with those classes.

That isolation and alienation can dehumanize the education experience, especially with regard to the relationship between students and professors. This is a well-documented problem in the literature (for example, Gillett-Swan, 2017) and, while scholars make recommendations for improvement, the problem proves difficult to solve. Beaudoin (2013) offered the following funny, but all too relatable anecdote to illustrate the issue:

Online students think that I am part of the computer sometimes. They type in a question, and they expect the machine to type back an answer right away. But maybe I'm in the midst of my commute, or teaching my three-hour class. When they don't get a reply for a few hours, they sometimes begin to panic, and send me repeat messages: 'Professor, I haven't gotten a reply yet!' (para 2)

I didn't demand immediate responses from my online professors, but the story of conflating humans and machines resonates. I was lucky to be in small enough online classes where I received personalized feedback from my faculty, but the lack of human interaction made it difficult to interpret that feedback at times. One professor was as warm and encouraging as one can be digitally, so it was not such an issue in her class. The other professor, however, had more of a direct and critical style. These are not bad qualities, but the online environment seemed to amplify the harshness of the feedback. Even worse, I couldn't really tell what he wanted without being able to talk to him in a way that allowed for the back and forth meaning construction enhanced by face-to-face communication. I probably could have scheduled an in-person meeting with him, but that didn't seem like an attractive option as our only interaction had been digital critique.

When I consider how few students take advantage of office hours under the best of circumstances, my lack of inclination to meet with this professor seems like a potentially important revelation. I lack a lot of the baggage that the other students in the class may have had in terms of feeling intimidated by faculty, not knowing how to talk to older people, etc., yet I still didn't go to office hours. In retrospect, I can see that the main reason for this is that I simply didn't feel as motivated in my online classes, which is a common problem (Bawa, 2016). It would be easy to chalk this up to personal responsibility and that is fair enough in my case as a 44-year-old professor taking some classes for personal enrichment. But I think it would be a mistake to lay the blame entirely at the feet of traditional age college students for underperforming in online classes. Students consistently complete online classes at lower rates than their in-person counterparts (Boton & Gregory, 2015) yet, we continue to grow the online sector, often at the expense of the live classroom.

The deleterious effects of online education on learning should be of greater concern to higher education leaders. Another less obvious, but related issue is the impact of online education on the human interaction between professor and student. It's hard to see what's missing from one's experience, but I felt the loss of opportunity that resulted from not knowing my online professors. Even the one who seemed a little harsh online might have been come across differently in person. Real life tends to round out aspects of our personality. Some of my colleagues are also short and direct in email, but that comes out more as friendly curmudgeon in person. I would imagine it's the same with struggling students; they may look hapless online, but present a more complex self in person. These may seem like nice, but not essential points until one considers how the decline in human interaction more generally is impacting the next generation.

SCREENS AND MENTAL HEALTH

Understanding how today's students experience the classroom necessitates some insight into their emotional lives more broadly. Twenge (2017) offers an in-depth analysis of what she calls, *iGen*, people born between 1995 and 2012. Based on extensive mixed-methods research, Twenge asserts that one of the defining trends of this generation is its lack of ability to deal with emotions. Raised by over-protective parents and glued to iPhones as children, these young people spent significantly less time engaged in both risk-taking and social interaction as compared to previous generations. Childhoods characterized by too much screen time and too little practice with real life-developmental tasks is resulting in a generation that never learned how to bounce back from setbacks or manage complex emotions. Twenge takes the argument further, suggesting that this generation has extended childhood for so long that they arrive on campus with remarkably less experience navigating adult experiences like dating and working.

Anyone who has worked on a college campus will likely relate to the examples of the mental health issues Twenge argues result from *iGen's* lack of practice with adult responsibilities. One consequence is that students arrive on campus feeling very unsure of themselves, which makes them less likely to engage with faculty. As Twenge explains, "It takes more reassurance and trust to get them to actively participate in class" (p. 307). Hence, the ability to evoke reassurance and trust is going to become an essential skill for professors if they are to teach this generation effectively.

Unfortunately, higher education is largely going in the opposite direction of what this generation needs in terms of a warm and supportive classroom environment. Instead of focusing institutional resources on faculty development in areas like contemplative pedagogy and other student-centered approaches to teaching, higher education leaders are continuing to promote more transition to online education. Technology has a place in higher education, but it is in danger of eclipsing universities' mission to provide students with the critical thinking skills necessary to participate in civic life as informed citizens. Echoing Noble (1977), Harari (2018) argues that we ought to invest at least as much in human minds as we do in artificial ones. Harari's point is part of a larger thesis about the importance of human capacity in sustaining democracy. Given the interdependence between education and liberty, the high stakes of this point cannot be overstated.

A vital part of maintaining the democratic purpose of education lies in refusing to let students be coopted for the benefit of serving a corporate elite. Students are people, which means they ought to be treated as ends in themselves, not means to other agendas. Fain (2017) points out how far higher education is straying from its agenda as a public good:

> Hence the scholarship on college student learning tends to be driven by corporate interests rather than character development. Policy makers frequently evoke future employers' wish lists when setting political agendas. In fact, the U.S. Chamber of Commerce developed a curriculum for government and higher education leaders to better assist employers as "end customers of a talent supply chain". (para 3)

The ethical problem here is hopefully abundantly clear, but it would be easy to miss the mental health connection. Fain's point about character development is an essential aspect of learning to which we need to return to address what has rightfully been called a mental health crisis in higher education given the 88% increase in severe psychiatric disorders reported on college campuses over the past five years (Pedrelli, Nyer, Yeung, Zulauf, & Wilens, 2015). While higher education leaders continue to hire more therapists, this is not a financially sustainable long-term plan. It's also not enough. Chang and Boyd (2016) speak to some studies indicating the limits of counseling centers in reducing unhappiness, pointing out that what do work are core beliefs in "something larger than the self" (p. 120). They are careful to point out that this something need not be religion, but meaning and purpose in a broader sense are necessary to human well-being.

HUMAN SOLUTIONS TO HUMAN CHALLENGES

While it's enticing to imagine software that will magically transform struggling students into college-ready wonders, I think we know in our hearts that this is wishful thinking. Anyone who has encountered the dreaded "support menu" on a generic phone line ("Press 1 for Billing Concerns, Press 2 for Shipping Issues," etc.) can intuit why this might be. Learning defies systemization because people are individuals. What is hard for me to understand about writing well, for example, might be easy for you and vice versa.

What helps is personal attention and that can't be given unless students have a chance to be heard. I can introduce a topic generally, but I can't say too much more about it until I listen how each student connects and/or fails to connect to the material. A great example of this occurs in a class I teach on attending skills. Students submit videos of themselves demonstrating building rapport, conveying empathy, etc. and then we watch them as a group. Each student identifies their strengths to build on and growth areas to address. There is a great deal of variation in the videos as students thrive and struggle with different aspects of attending skills. The level of engagement in this class is consistently high because students report feeling like they are an active part of the learning. The class is delightfully unpredictable because each new group of students contributes their own knowledge and experience to the collective enterprise.

When students struggle, I try to help them personally, not bureaucratically, an important distinction Noddings (2013) makes in the context of what it means to truly care about students:

> We establish funds, or institutions, or agencies in order to provide the caretaking we judge to be necessary. The original impulse is often the one associated with caring. It arises in individuals. But as groups of individuals discuss the perceived needs of another individual or group, the imperative changes from "I must do something" to "Something must be done." This change is accompanied by a shift from the nonrational and subjective to the rational and objective. What should be done? Who should do it?

Why should the persons named do it? This sort of thinking is not in itself a mistake; it is needed. But it has buried within it the seed of major error. The danger is that caring, which is essentially nonrational in that it requires a constitutive engrossment and displacement of motivation, may gradually or abruptly be transformed into abstract problem solving. There is, then, a shift of focus from the cared-for to the "problem". (p. 25)

I benefited from this ethic of care many years ago when I submitted my first scholarly work for publication. My work was not good, but University of Vermont Professor Emerita, Dr. Kathleen Manning, then the Executive Editor of the *Journal of Student Affairs Research and Practice*, took what had to be a considerable amount of time to explain in detail what I needed to do to make the manuscript publishable. She did not "dumb it down," but she did articulate the issues in ways that someone new to the enterprise could actually understand. This is the kind of attitude and commitment that reflect higher education at its best.

CONCLUSION

I should be used to it by now, but it continues to astonish me that many higher education leaders keep trying to automate learning. Education is a fundamentally relational enterprise impervious to standardization. Students need professors to make the content come alive in meaningful ways. They need models of how the theoretical shows up in real life. This is how students connect to ideas and let them inspire their own thinking.

An example of this occurred on my campus last year when a professor (Dr. Dan West) invited his Introduction to Human Communication students to ask him any question they wanted. In a class session on love and relationships, a student asked him how he knew his wife was "the one." Inspired by his heartfelt answer, a student Tweeted it and within hours, the Tweet went viral with 76,000 Retweets (Chen, 2017).

It would be easy to overlook the meaning in this story, dismissing it as a cute anecdote about romantic love, but that would be an oversimplification. I think this interaction became a story because it tapped into the longing students have for an education that evokes. West let the students into his life a bit, sharing a part of himself that evoked something in that precise moment. Follett (1924) writes of this connection as the ultimate goal in being present with one another:

All human interaction should be the evocation by each from the other of new forms of undreamed of before, and all intercourse that is not evocation should be eschewed. Release, evocation by release, release by evocation-this is the fundamental law of the universe. (p. 137)

According to Bain's (2011) research on effective college teachers, this ability to evoke is part of what makes for excellent teaching. Evocation rooted in self-disclosure is particularly important when it comes to struggle; students benefit from faculty who can articulate how they moved from not understanding something to beginning to grasp it. Those examples help both emotionally and intellectually which, as discussed in the previous chapters, turn out to be inseparable. The ability to speak to this intersection of affect and cognition will be vital as we move forward in the vast majority of public higher education institutions where the successful implementation of an access mission will be crucial for long-term viability. This theme of a future built on meaningful access will be the focus of the next chapter.

References

Bain, K. (2011). *What the best college teachers do*. Cambridge, MA: Harvard University Press.

Bateson, M. (1989). *Composing a life*. New York, NY: Grove Press.

Bawa, P. (2016). Retention in online courses: Exploring issues and solutions—A literature review. *Sage Open, 6*(1), 1–11.

Beaudoin, P. (2013, March 26). Managing your online time. *Chronicle of Higher Education*. Retrieved from https://www.chronicle.com/article/Managing-Your-Online-Time/138153.

Boroditsky, L. (2011). How language shapes thought. *Scientific American, 304*(2), 62–65.

Boton, E. C., & Gregory, S. (2015). Minimizing attrition in online degree courses. *Journal of Educators Online, 12*(1), 62–90.

Carr, N. (2011). *The shallows: What the Internet is doing to our brains*. New York, NY: W. W. Norton.

Chang, H., & Boyd, D. (2016). *Spirituality in higher education: Autoethnographies*. New York, NY: Routledge.

Chen, T. (2017). A student asked their professor how you know you're in love, and his touching answer has gone viral. *BuzzFeed News*. Retrieved from https://www.buzzfeednews.com/article/tanyachen/my-professor-avoids-making-eye-contact-w-me-in-public.

Dimeo, J. (2017, April 12). Counting online students. *Inside Higher Education*. Retrieved from https://www.insidehighered.com/digital-learning/article/2017/04/12/report-documents-3-year-change-online-enrollments.

Fain, P. (2017, October 17). Curriculum for work-force development. *Inside Higher Education*. Retrieved from https://www.insidehighered.com/quicktakes/2017/10/17/curriculum-work-force-development.

Foer, F. (2017). *World without mind: The existential threat of big tech*. New York, NY: Penguin Books.

Follett, M. P. (1924). *Creative experience*. New York, NY: Longmans, Green and Company.

Gazzaley, A., & Rosen, L. (2016). *The distracted mind: Ancient brains in a high-tech world*. Cambridge: MIT Press.

Gillett-Swan, J. (2017). The challenges of online learning: Supporting and engaging the isolated learner. *Journal of Learning Design, 10*(1), 20–30.

Giroux, H. A. (2015). *University in chains: Confronting the military-industrial-academic complex*. New York, NY: Routledge.

Harari, Y. (2018, October). Why technology favors tyranny. *The Atlantic*. Retrieved from https://www.theatlantic.com/magazine/archive/2018/10/yuval-noah-harari-technology-tyranny/568330/.

Harrison, L. M. (in press). Using technology in teaching. In L. Flores & J. Olcott (Eds.), *The academic's handbook*. Durham, NC: Duke University Press.

Harrison, L. M., & Mather, P. (2015). *Alternative solutions to higher education's problems: An appreciative approach to reform*. New York, NY: Routledge.

McLuhan, M. (1964). *Understanding media: The extensions of man*. Cambridge: MIT press.

Noble, D. (1977). *America by design: Science, technology, and the rise of corporate capitalism*. Oxford, UK: Oxford University Press.

Noddings, N. (2013). *Caring: A relational approach to ethics and moral education*. Berkeley, CA: University of California Press.

Pedrelli, P., Nyer, M., Yeung, A., Zulauf, C., & Wilens, T. (2015). College students: Mental health problems and treatment considerations. *Academic Psychiatry, 39*(5), 503–511.

Pinker, S. (2014). *The village effect: How face-to-face contact can make us healthier, happier, and smarter*. Toronto, ON: Random House Canada.

Powers, W. (2010). *Hamlet's BlackBerry: Building a good life in the digital age*. New York: HarperCollins.

Rosen, L., Carrier, L. M, & Cheever, N. (2013). Facebook and texting made me do it: Media induced task switching while studying. *Computers in Human Behavior, 29*(3), 948–958.

Seltzer, L., Prososki, A., Ziegler, T., & Pollack, S. (2012). Instant messages vs. speech: Hormones and why we still need to hear each other. *Evolution and Human Behavior, 33*(1), 42–45.

Shahjahan, R., Wagner, A., & Wane, N. (2009). Rekindling the sacred: Toward a decolonizing pedagogy in higher education. *Journal of Thought, 44*(1), 59–75.

Twenge, J. (2017). *IGen: Why today's super-connected kids are growing up less rebellious, more tolerant, less happy—and completely unprepared for adulthood—and what that means for the rest of us.* New York, NY: Simon and Schuster.

Weil, S. (1952). *Gravity and grace.* New York, NY: G.P. Putnam's Sons.

CHAPTER 6

Making College Better

Abstract In this chapter, I call for a renewed commitment to expanding access to higher education for all students, including those who struggle. True access requires greater institutional resources allocated to the work of helping all students to thrive. With the current 6-year graduation rates remaining stagnant at 59%, universities ought to have both ethical and pragmatic reasons to prioritize struggling students. That said, culture change is slow and educators cannot wait for systemic overhaul when they have students sitting in front of them this semester. Hence, this chapter concludes with concrete, practical strategies educators can employ in the short-time while working toward long-term structural improvement.

Keywords Prioritization · Slow scholarship · High touch · Feedback · Success

My second student career ended unceremoniously as I picked up my official certificate in the Linguistics Department one afternoon toward the end of August, 2017. The Administrative Assistant checked my name off a list and handed it to me with a kind, "Congratulations." It was a small thing, but I was grateful to her for the acknowledgment. I smiled back and thanked her.

The certificate now hangs on my faculty office wall. I joke that I worked harder to earn that piece of paper than the graduate diplomas

© The Author(s) 2019
L. M. Harrison, *Teaching Struggling Students*,
https://doi.org/10.1007/978-3-030-13012-1_6

next to it. While that's not entirely true, I do identify my TEFL certificate as the most unique of my credentials. I learned more by being a student than I could have imagined. What follows are some recommendations about university teaching and learning rooted in the insights I gained from being a struggling student.

In the introduction, I confessed that I had not thought about the audience enough when writing my previous books. Fortunately, I did not make that mistake in this book, imagining the reader many times as an integral part of my writing process. The audience played an especially big role in how I approached this chapter. I imagined a reader somewhat like myself before I became a student. There are two primary qualities that matter most for the purposes of this chapter. First, I conceptualized the reader as a good person who cares about all students, but has a limited understanding of what to do with those who struggle. I have focused on this aspect throughout the entirety of the book and will provide some takeaways on this point toward the end of the chapter. Second, I imagined the reader as a educator fairly devoted to teaching, but stretched too thin. One can enhance their skill in working with struggling students effectively, but this will prove futile if they don't have the time to enact this capacity.

In retrospect, I can see that I was burned out as a professor when I started the TEFL program. I loved teaching and was tired of fighting so hard for the time and energy to do it well. I still have to fight, but hopefully more fruitfully now that I've at least named the problem and developed some strategies to address it. In this chapter, I will identify and discuss these strategies in hopes of providing insight as we move forward in teaching struggling students more effectively.

PRIORITIZE STRUGGLING STUDENTS FOR BOTH ETHICAL AND PRACTICAL REASONS

I ended the last chapter by arguing that we ought to focus on implementing the vision of an access mission in public higher education. Though "access" may be the biggest buzzword in higher education, we are ambivalent at best. Nowhere is this ambivalence more clear than in the relentless concern about rankings. Despite complaints about their legitimacy, rankings dominate too many higher education leaders' agendas because they believe higher placement leads to competitive advantage.

There are many flaws in this argument, which I have detailed elsewhere (see Harrison & Price, 2017). The main problem for our purposes here is that this hyperfocus on rankings leads to an institutional culture in which struggling students are neglected. While universities lavish resources on the National Merit Scholar crowd, students on the lower end of the academic ladder receive less attention. Universities tend to address their challenges bureaucratically, largely through early detection software and student affairs professionals who meet with students on academic proba-tion. These efforts have merit, but they are not the same thing as the care-ful cultivation enjoyed by students recruited for their academic prowess.

This discrepancy is an equity issue, but it's also a practical one. There is a finite supply of high achieving, well-resourced youth seeking to fill the slots in public higher education institutions. The far larger popu-lation of young people are non college-ready students who attended under-resourced schools, but they are not as desirable due to the rank-ings game. The rankings issue is part of a bigger problem Kerr (1963) named many years ago in his coining of the term *multiversity*. The idea is that institutional time, attention, and resources are spread too thin as business and political interests eclipse educational ones, resulting in organizations that are "multi" purposed rather than focused singularly on educating the next generation.

Braskamp, Trautvetter, and Ward's (2016) study of 500 church-affiliated colleges suggest that there is an alternative to too many com-peting priorities inhibiting our ability to give struggling students the time and attention they need. Despite the considerable diversity of col-leges represented in the study, the findings indicated remarkably consist-ent student-centered missions:

> More specifically, all of these colleges are committed to developing their students holistically. They feel that their mission is to assist students to know themselves—who they are and their purpose in life—to be self-aware in this global life; to develop their intellectual abilities, to cultivate social, civic, and moral responsibilities; and to examine faith claims. In other words, holistic student learning and development are both reflected in the college's mission and are taken seriously. (p. 45)

The authors were careful to point out that these were not "contrived" (p. 44) missions reminiscent of those panned in movies and TV shows about the banality of business-speak. These missions were integral to the campuses included in the study from how faculty were hired to how budgets were allocated. It's not that these campuses never had issues or conflicts, but they benefited from a shared understanding of what should be driving priorities.

It is usually at about this point in the argument that claims of realism are made. The argument is something along the lines of, yes, it would be nice to focus on the holistic development of students, but economic pressures create the need for ever-increasing enrollments. These enrollments typically come in the form of larger classes and more online offerings. If this system were working, I would have a hard time disputing it. But the truth is that we've been trying these strategies for years in higher education and they have proven largely ineffective. We continue to experience both financial strain and stagnant retention and graduation rates. It's time to admit that running the university like a factory is failing.

Leaders in the colleges profiled in Braskamp et al. (2016) study were not blindly idealistic. They were very aware of their competition and worked diligently to promote and protect their brand. They were savvy enough to see that what's best for the student is actually also best for the institution. When colleges invest in creating meaningful educational experiences for students, they see a return on that investment both in terms of being able to prioritize human and financial resources more intelligently, and also in the form of loyal donors.

It would be easy to dismiss this research as not widely applicable due to its focus on church-affiliated colleges. This would be unwise on a few counts, the main one being that the ability to be mission-driven is not exclusive to the religious realm. It will be difficult for higher education leaders to address this issue of mission creep, but faculty do not have to wait for that to happen in order to start prioritizing struggling students in their own work.

COMMIT TO A CLEARER IDENTITY ROOTED IN TEACHING

I recently attended a dissertation defense where issues in community journalism comprised the research. The student spoke eloquently about the strong sense of identity among journalists, particularly regarding the concept of the fourth estate as a unifying construct. It occurred to me that higher education lacks this clear idea and that the lack of consensus about what we ought to be doing in colleges and universities has real consequences.

Chickering (2003), for example, articulated a worrisome trend of faculty's detachment from students in the contemporary university. The literature is replete with both direct and indirect references to this phenomenon, linking it to a range of issues. Some scholars point to the lack of adequate preparation for college teaching as the culprit (Robinson & Hope, 2013). Others lay the blame on the corporatization of higher education, which demands that faculty spend more time procuring grants and producing research than focusing on students (Boyer, Moser, & Braxton, 2015). Based on my own experience and conversations with other faculty, these and other factors contribute to a near constant feeling of never being able to focus on what matters to them. While a certain degree of stress is to be expected in most positions, it seems to me that our particular brand of pressure in academia stems from lack of commitment to a core purpose from which all activities ought to flow.

Helping struggling students to succeed has to be part of that core purpose. First, struggling students are the new normal in most universities that have shifted from elite enterprises to access institutions. While many universities still behave as if college-ready young people comprise the majority of their student bodies, this is no longer the case. Coupled with the fact that extreme inequality has taken a profoundly negative toll on many K-12 schools, many of today's students enter college without the skills of their predecessors. Whether fan or foe of the idea of college for all, the expansion of college going necessitates making the shift in understanding that the new work of faculty is learning to be effective with a mostly non college-ready student population.

Prioritizing struggling students is what's right for both the students themselves as well as our institutions' financial viability. It's also what's best for us as faculty. The academic life offers many benefits, but the near constant demands on our time have serious consequences for our mental health. Astin and Astin (1999) conducted one of the seminal studies on faculty stress; "the university owns my life now" (p. 22) is one of the oft-quoted lines from a participant in their study. I've had this same feeling many times, despite the protections of tenure and a reasonable amount of positive self-regard.

Many laud and even resent the flexibility of the academic schedule, but they fail to realize that boundlessness comes with a cost. While it's true that faculty can leave their offices in the middle of the day without punching a clock, it's equally true that we can literally work all the time. The nature of our work is never-ending; there is always another article to be written or a reference letter to submit or a committee project to be maintained. Some of us overwork due to our own personality peculiarities, but many of us do so because the academic culture increasingly demands it. Much of the blame for this problem has been rightly placed on decreased public funding and the increased pressures that result. Our strategy in those cases has to be systemic change. But we must also examine our own complicity in buying into a system that pits us against each other in a cage fight for grants, perks, etc.

Some faculty are starting to push back on the incivility that results from this excessively competitive environment. Dowland and Pérez (2018) wrote a piece warning about the toxicity of understanding one's academic standing as so precarious that it makes people selfish with their time and energy. They advocate a more generous spirit, such as willingness to mentor students, write reference letters, and help others with publications. They rightfully frame these acts as radical, linking the personal with political change. I found this to be the strength of the piece because we too often feel helpless in the face of structural barriers. I do not seek to minimize the often formidable challenges of behaving counter-culturally. Yet, if we waited for systemic improvement, nothing would ever get done. The only way for change to happen is for people to start to change in the here and now.

There are always time and bandwidth challenges, but I've noticed rich rewards in my own life as a result of focusing more intentionally on mentoring struggling students. Unfortunately, these rewards never come from the institution in terms of merit pay, course releases, or any of the other mechanisms put in place to incentivize faculty. I'm not naïve enough to think that I will reap material rewards for spending energy on an institutionally undervalued activity. I also know that this doesn't mean the activity is not worth doing anyway.

To be clear, I am not a martyr in any way. So, I am not suggesting that readers devote themselves in some saintly way to the underappreciated work of helping struggling students. I do believe this work should be rewarded more fairly and that we have to work for systemic change. But in the meantime, we have the students sitting in front of us this semester. And as importantly, we have our own hearts and minds to consider. Scholarship and service are important; I'm not recommending their elimination. They should not, however, make so many demands on our time that we are too exhausted to demonstrate care in teaching. Students notice when we're not present, as evidenced in this simple, but powerful story in Berg and Seeber's (2016) account of a professor's surprise at the level of students' gratitude for a simple expression of care:

> At the end of the class I was surrounded by people saying "Thank you for listening," "Thank you for noticing that we are there-or, rather, when we are not." I received more emails later thanking me for caring. It made me quite glum to realize that we often plough on no matter what's going on in the room. (p. 45)

The professor's insight about ploughing on struck me because I used to do it all the time. I am better about it now, but still struggle to not lose sight of students in the daily grind of academia. Fortunately, there are ways to reprioritize our time and attention by tapping into the countercultural spirit that inspired many of our academic careers in the first place.

Make Time to Work with Struggling Students

I will admit that I felt like a hypocrite many times during the writing of this book. There is a famous psychological experiment that serves as a good metaphor for the hypocrisy. As the story goes, people moving between two points encountered a person in need of help. Subjects who were given time pressure were less likely to stop and help, regardless of having recently heard a talk about the story of the Good Samaritan (Darley & Batson, 1973). The moral of the story is that we can become so focused on a task that we forget the substance of what's important.

I had similar moments where I was exasperated by actual struggling students needing my attention when I was trying to focus on writing about struggling students. I share this experience as a gesture of solidarity with teachers from preschool through graduate school who struggle themselves to meet the needs of students who seek our time and attention. We're increasingly stretched thin as those who never or rarely teach themselves demand greater "efficiencies," often in the form of larger enrollments and/or shifts to online education. Most of those who teach view it as a calling and went into the profession to work with students. Yet, the pressures of the structures in which we work can make it feel impossible to do the labor intensive and largely unrewarded work required to help struggling students.

It's clear that we must work diligently to challenge the policies and practices that create the time scarcity in the first place. Similarly, reward structures must be re-examined in order to align with a prioritization of helping struggling students. Recommendations to change the system are often true, but also frustrating because we can't always do that in the immediate future. So, while it's important to play the long game, I think we also need to be more critical in our relationship with time right now in the present. Shahjahan (2015) offers a useful alternative to understanding time as a linear commodity that we should monitor and control from a scarcity perspective. For example, I suspect that most faculty believe we spend too much of our time in meetings and on email. Particularly for those of us with tenure, we can push back on what counts as time well spent and reallocate this time to working with struggling students.

I hold no illusions that this choice is a consequence-free one. Working with struggling students takes time that is difficult to quantify. Volumes have been written about the lack of reward for teaching in the academy (Hersh & Merrow, 2015); the largely invisible and unquantifiable labor one dedicates to struggling students is even less acknowledged. I have paid the price myself in terms of political fallout like diminished merit pay and judgment about refusing some administrative tasks. These realities frustrate me and I do what I can to confront them.

Despite the consequences and frustrations, I still find that the benefits outweigh the costs when it comes to prioritizing struggling students in how I plan my time. The simple truth is that working with them is more rewarding than just about anything else I do in my life. I can't adequately describe the fulfillment that comes from helping students to find their voice in writing, for example, especially when they have been told all their life that they're just not good at it. As Palmer (2017) eloquently put it, "The university is a place where we grant respect to only a few things—to the text, to the expert, to those who win in competition. But we do not grant respect to students, to stumbling and failing" (p. 20). When I reclaimed my right to grant respect in accordance with my own values, I reconnected with the passion that made me want to teach in the first place.

All of this is to say that the first step in teaching struggling students more effectively is to carve out the time to do it. Unless we want to endanger our own mental health, this process will likely require cutting out some current responsibilities in order to make room for a new priority.

I realize that this prospect is much easier said than done, so I offer a story to illustrate that it is possible. I was sitting in a meeting recently where it was clear that nothing was actually going to be accomplished. Like most people, I usually endure these situations by playing on my laptop or staring out the window, but I realized in that moment that these were behaviors I needed to unlearn. If we collectively started to reclaim our time and allocate it to the more important work of teaching, we would not live in such a constant state of time scarcity.

In that particular moment, I was thinking about all the papers I had to grade and the time it takes to do that well. I could have easily chosen to stay in the meeting and cut corners on the grading, which would have been the more politically expedient thing to do. No one would have been the wiser if I'd written "Nice Job!" or "Needs Work" on my students' papers and called it a day. It seems like such an inconsequential thing, but the cumulative effect of not prioritizing our time is making us less effective with struggling students than we could be. Students need clear, thoughtful, and personalized feedback to build on their strengths and address their growth areas. In addition, I need the satisfaction that comes with doing the work I was hired to do instead of sitting in a meeting where I was clearly not needed.

So, I got up and left. I felt almost heroic, like one of the few people who refused to participate in the Milgram Experiment. I went back to my office and graded papers, recalling the many times students told me I was the first professor who gave them meaningful feedback on an assignment. I know I'm not a better person than their previous professors; I'm just the one who left the meeting. I'm aware that the ability to enact even a minor rebellion requires some degree of political calculation. I spent the first part of my scholarly career studying how people negotiate power in academia, so I realize there can be consequences for choosing one's own values over that of the institution. I recommend resisting at whatever level you deem safe, recalibrating your choices as conditions change. There is also the important issue of being ethical in one's choices by not dumping less desirable work on junior faculty and/ or graduate students. Yet, there is also a risk in not pushing back and reclaiming the time it takes to due diligence to students, particularly the ones who need more attention.

If you can repurpose some of your time to focus on struggling students, you really are halfway there. The next step is to develop some strategies, which I'll focus on for the remainder of this chapter.

EMBRACE THE TRUTH THAT LEARNING
IS WHAT DEFINES HUMAN BEINGS

Part of the issue in teaching struggling students is that too often, they are conceptualized as simply not smart. It seems like a small thing, but this mental model greatly inhibits one's capacity to work effectively with them. We've all heard the old adage that teachers have to believe their students are capable of learning to be able to teach them, but there are times when this is difficult to buy. Even though we know intellectually that we ourselves find some subjects more intuitive than others, it's still hard to grasp student struggle with our own discipline for some reason.

I have found understanding all students as capable of learning to be essential in my own ability to teach struggling students. I was surprised by how much making this small mental shift mattered in becoming more effective as a teacher. It's not that I thought students were not smart before, but being in institutional cultures obsessed with rankings, stand-ardized test scores, and all the other familiar ways of sorting students dis-torted my perceptions. Unwittingly, my theory in use had become that some students simply lacked the intelligence and/or motivation to do the work and that I was therefore not responsible for them. Although I would have espoused a different theory, my practice was something along the lines of "you can lead a horse to water, but you cannot make it drink."

A few years ago, I revived a course on college teaching and began doing a lot of reading on pedagogy in the process of redesigning it. I came across an interview with Mary Catherine Bateson in which she identified learning as the very definition of humanity:

> You've heard stories about the people that wanted to raise a lion in their home, people that have wanted to raise a chimp in their home; other sto-ries of trying to tame a wild animal, and when it matures, it loses its flex-ibility, and the relationship breaks down...in (contrast)...human beings remain childlike. They're open to new learning and even very deep learn-ing that changes your personality, really. Right through the life cycle, human beings remain playful — and play is a very important part of learn-ing — and experimental. Most other species, they figure out how to be a rabbit or a chicken or an owl or a fish, and that's what they do for the rest of their life; so learning is us. (para 52)

I remind myself of Bateson's words whenever I feel tempted to give up on a student. I realize now that most of my frustration has more to do with my own teaching challenges than students' struggle. Part of over-coming the hurdle is being kinder with ourselves. Teaching is hard work that burns people out. Sometimes we blame students rather than owning the challenge of conveying the material.

I used to think faculty (including myself) who complained about stu-dents' under-performance were being impatient, mean, and/or arrogant. This is sometimes the case. Also, there are times when the onus is on the students. But I also think faculty frustration with ourselves is an under-appreciated aspect of the student underperformance dilemma. When I'm so self-critical that a student's failure to grasp what I'm saying threatens my identity as a competent professor, I'm likely to frame the problem in terms of blame. Not wanting to blame myself, it's easier to blame the stu-dent. I also have a tendency toward a control paradigm in this situation, demanding the student either work harder or accept the consequences.

Rogers' (1995) construct of unconditional positive regard is instruc-tive as an attitude that expands our possibilities beyond blame and con-trol. When I hold both myself and students in unconditional positive regard, it's easier to be tolerant toward shortcomings wherever they lie. That tolerance allows me to stick with both students and myself as we work though issues together. Unconditional positive regard is some-times mistaken as a character trait presumably only found in people who are extra nice. Fortunately, unconditional positive regard is better understood as an orientation that can be chosen. As with any individual choice, environmental conditions either help or hinder one's ability to sustain it. Environments that allow time and space for the cultivation of relationships enhance our capacity for patience, an essential component in unconditional positive regard. Conversely, environments dictated by coldness and competitiveness do not make it easy for faculty to do the work it takes to operate from a place of unconditional positive regard. Hence, one of the longer term projects in making substantive gains with struggling students has to be challenging long-established norms in higher education, beginning with our addiction to speed.

RECLAIM THE WORK OF CARING THROUGH THE SLOW SCHOLARSHIP MOVEMENT

One of the more bizarre contradictions I see in higher education right now is the valorization of student centeredness coupled with nearly zero reward for the care work that involves. We can buy as many software badging systems, early alert warnings, and other costly technology products we want, but nothing will replace the work of actually caring about students. Much of this care work falls on women and faculty of color who are expected to mentor students without additional compensation for doing so. This puts us in a Catch-22 of sorts, wanting neither to abandon students nor being act like pushovers presenting as attractive options.

There is a third way, advocated by those who appropriate aspects of the slow food movement and apply them to higher education. Using the slow food movement as a model, the idea is to reprioritize quality over quantity when it comes to all aspects of faculty life. Rather than allowing oneself to feel constantly pulled between the competing demands of scholarship, teaching, and service, "slow scholars" call for a re-evaluation of these unrealistic expectations. Mountz et al. (2015), for example, critically analyzes the ways in which the hyper focus on faculty productivity marginalizes care work that cannot be captured by software like the Digital Measures her and my university demand we use. When we obsess over metrics, our work is diminished as an individual counting game of publications, grant applications, weighted student credit hours, advisees, and the like. Our ability to rack up high numbers is often closely connected to how efficient we are in screening out the work that is less difficult to capture on a spreadsheet.

One of the aims of the slow scholarship movement is to create more balanced assessments that tell the stories behind the numbers. What does it matter if I have 25 advisees if I don't know their names or their intellectual interests? What if our CVs included the time we spent talking to students about what they aspire to in this life and the thank you notes they sent us about what those conversations meant to them? Systems feel like "just the way things are," but they are human-made constructions and therefore changeable.

In addition to advocating for slow scholarship for ourselves, we must fight back against what Hartman and Darab (2012) refer to as "speedy pedagogy." Speedy pedagogy is that form of information transmittal that occurs in shallow sound bites, often in the disembodied form of online education. This approach is lauded for its cheap and fast delivery much in the same way that fast food once was until critical scholars pointed out the nutritional poverty of empty calories. If the factory approach to higher education produced better outcomes, it would be difficult to argue against it. The reality is that 6-year graduation rates for students at public universities remain stagnant at just under 60% (NCES, 2018).

Coupled with recent criticism about higher education not doing enough to expand economic opportunities for low-income students (Fischer, 2016), we can make a strong case for abandoning the speedy pedagogy approach.

Higher education institutions that consistently demonstrate the best records for fostering student success prioritize time for meaningful faculty-student interaction (Kuh, Kinzie, Schuh, Whitt, & Associates, 2008). Yet, only 22% of students can identify a mentor that helped them to achieve their goals during their time in college (Ray & Kafka, 2014). Without personalized guidance, students flounder. As one professor articulated about helping students who struggle with writing, "The only thing that really works with novice writers is getting to spend time writing and talking to somebody about their writing" (Duncheon, 2015). The professor was speaking in contrast to an efficiency initiative that had been put into place that was largely ineffective because literacy occurs slowly and as the result of interaction, two features absent from the remediation program (p. 158).

We can thus make the case for slow scholarship on both ethical and pragmatic grounds. We would serve our students more effectively by prioritizing humane education and recover some of our own mental health in the process. If faculty were less depleted, we would have more to give our students.

Advocate for Less High Tech and More High Touch

I was sitting with a student who was struggling on a writing project one afternoon when I noticed how bleary eyed she looked staring furtively at her laptop. I asked her if I could close the computer. Her expression was one of puzzlement, but she said okay. I then took her pen and notepad and asked her to pretend there was no paper to be written, just tell me what she wanted to say. She verbalized about 10 minutes of truly brilliant thinking while I took notes. I handed them back to her and she looked stunned. She praised me and I told her truthfully that all I did was write down what she said. She ended up writing an excellent paper.

If a student reaches out their hand, I say it's okay to hold it. I don't know if it was always this way, but it seems to me that we've gotten rather cold in the academy and maybe society in general. Rather than freaking out over helicopter parenting and how we're so busy, I'd rather do what has been proven time and time again to be effective. I know when I struggled in my Linguistic classes, just a little encouragement from professors brought out my best work.

Professors' use of warm language was a significant finding in Bain's (2011) research on effective college teaching. It may seem like a small thing, but the ability to be relatable matters to students. Simply using students' names and greeting them warmly inculcates a sense of safety. They breathe a little easier when we make them comfortable which, in turn, empowers them to be a little more vulnerable with us. When students are willing to be vulnerable, they are more likely to admit struggle rather than trying to hide it. In the absence of vulnerability, students can be defensive in the face of struggle. I've seen this phenomenon many times in my higher education career. There is the occasional student who is too closed off to reach, but I've found that the overwhelming majority of students respond positively to a high touch approach.

When students are treated like a number, they understandably withdraw. This is particularly true for struggling students. My experience as a struggling student made me realize how I glossed over the lower performing students in my own classroom. I knew the high achieving students better because I could relate to them more easily. We had a lot in common, so those were the students whom I knew as individuals. The most the lower performing students got from me were generic invitations like "Any questions?" and directives to come to office hours. The few who were brave enough to come to office hours probably did not get a lot of help as I repeated my "What questions do you have?" and "What is unclear?" prompts. It's not that I didn't want to help, but I didn't see how monumentally unhelpful those questions were until I was on the other side of them.

What I learned from being on the other side of those questions is this: If students could answer those questions, they wouldn't be struggling in the first place. When struggling students come to office hours now, I say something more along the lines of, "I'm going to present you with the greatest hits of things students tend to struggle with in this class. If your issue is one of these things, great. If not, we'll keep digging away at it until we figure it out." I've watched students breathe literal sighs of relief as the result of this approach. First, it signals that they are not the first student to not immediately comprehend everything that is going on in the class. Second, this approach conveys that I'm not totally clueless about how to help students grasp the material. Finally, and perhaps most importantly, this approach conveys a sense of alliance.

Students need to hear us frame struggle as a puzzle to be worked through together, not a sentence they must serve in isolation. I don't diminish their concerns, but I do try to model a sense of lighthearted-ness about it so they can approach struggle with more confidence and less trepidation.

GIVE MORE FEEDBACK; DO LESS GRADING

What would it look like to be more successful with struggling students? I know one thing that did not help in my experience of being a strug-gling student was the grade. The 67%s were disheartening and the 100%s were meaningless. Grades function as carrots and sticks, which would seem on the surface to be effective. Yet, the stick element creates a cer-tain amount of anxiety that leads to more gaming than learning (Pope, 2008). Nowhere is this more evident than in the rampant cheating increasingly occurring on college campuses today. I witnessed some of this academic dishonesty myself in my first class. I was surprised by how much I wrestled with whether to report it because I empathized with the student.

I felt torn between justice and mercy in this case, but the bigger ques-tion is what leads students to cheat in the first place. Some of it can be chalked up to poor character, but some suggest that the recent increase has more to do with anxiety about the role grades might play in one's future prospects in an uncertain world. When we turn up the heat on rankings and competition, it should not be surprising that some students will focus more on the extrinsic reward than learning the material. An increase in cheating seems to be one of the consequences for making education into a game.

The carrot function of grades also seems less effective than one might think due to its use as an extrinsic reward. Intrinsic rewards consistently outperform extrinsic ones in terms of successful motivation. There is something about the trinket of the extrinsic reward that seems to dimin-ish the satisfaction that comes purely from the desire to do it. Recent neuroscience research challenges the rigid behaviorism of the past that asserted motivation as simple drives toward pleasure and away from pain (Di Domenico & Ryan, 2017). Researchers are finding that people per-form optimally when driven not by instrumentalism, but their "inherent human capacities for psychological growth, engagement, and wellness" (Ryan & Deci, 2017, p. 3).

The ability to access this research hinges on our understanding that all students can learn, that this capacity is what defines us as humans. Without this belief in what's inside a student, it's easy to misunderstand the nature of good teaching. If we think struggling students are just not smart, we're tempted to approach them as empty vessels into which we try to force the consumption of knowledge through carrots and sticks. If we understand that all people have the potential for intellectual curiosity and expansion, then we know that it's always best to work with what's inside the student.

The main idea in the new research on motivation is that people learn not from an outside entity demanding it from them using a system of punishments and rewards, but by accessing their inherent capacity for growth. This is not a passive phenomenon that simply happens, but one that can be cultivated by teaching people to order their consciousness in such a way as to maximize the potential for what Csikszentmihalyi (2008) called *flow*. As Csikszentmihalyi explained, "flow is the way people describe their state of mind when consciousness is harmoniously ordered, and they want to pursue whatever they are doing for its own sake" (p. 6). One of the conditions required for this harmonious consciousness is a tolerance for stretching oneself, the idea being that too much self-consciousness inhibits the ability to lose oneself in one's work.

In my experience, grades are the death knell of students' willingness to stretch themselves. In their minds, low grades translate to less desirability in the job and/or graduate school markets. Whether this is true or not, it is the general belief by both students and parents whose pressure has created a great deal of grade inflation. Many universities are now fighting grade inflation out of a concern that grades have lost their meaning. I have received this message from multiple institutions, both directly and indirectly. Directly, I was encouraged to "protect the integrity of the A" by issuing less of those in a curve-style grading system. Indirectly, I am now required to let the university know how many A's, B's, etc. I am issuing, the tacit understanding being that my positive course evaluations will mean more if I still get them while issuing worse grades.

Instead of investing this much time and energy into bean counting, why not accept this current moment as an opportunity to evolve? Instead of reducing the beautifully complex phenomenon of learning to a single letter or number, why not write a paragraph about each student's strengths and growth areas at the end of a semester? How much more meaningful would that be than a letter or number that often ends up being arbitrary anyway? I'm teaching a class right now in which I return students' work with comments, not grades. They express a lot of appreciation for personalized responses to what they're saying. This approach does not compromise standards. I make it clear that those who don't make an effort should think twice about coming to me for independent study opportunities, letters of recommendation and/or job leads. But I also make it clear that effort is the currency in my classes, not some absolute standard that denies the fact that humans are wonderfully varied and therefore impervious to standardization.

Why not eliminate barriers to students' natural capacities for learning, focusing less on external rewards like grades and more on internal motivators like the potential to build a meaningful life? This may sound idealistic, but the fact is that the current system is not working all that well. Higher education leaders talk about innovation and change, yet seem reticent to examine critically some of the very practices that undermine student learning. Part of the problem seems to be a distorted notion of what success looks like, a theme that I will examine in the next section.

Redefine Success

Success must be redefined in terms of how far a student travels from where they started rather than a finish line toward which some students receive a wildly unfair head start. I present the following figure to demonstrate the flawed thinking in measuring students only in terms of where they land with little consideration to where they began (Fig. 6.1).

In an uncritical understanding of student success, Y students are the big winners because they landed at the furthest point. In this framework, colleges should recruit as many Y students as they can to demonstrate the prestige of their student population. I argue that X students represent the more substantive achievement to which universities ought to strive. While Y students may have landed further ahead, they travelled very little to get there. College did not make much of a difference for Y students who were already very far down the line by the time they finished high school. For X students, however, college made a huge difference. If one focuses on the journey rather than the destination, it is clear that college is more transformative for X students.

A related idea can be found in McNair, Albertine, Cooper, McDonald, and Major's (2016) book, *Becoming a Student-Ready*

Fig. 6.1   Student success as distance travelled

College: A New Culture of Leadership for Student Success. In this work, the authors advocate for shifting the paradigm from college-ready students to student-ready colleges. Rather than engaging in an arms race of sorts for the "better" students, why not work more effectively with all students? This is both the right thing to do in terms of promoting higher education's public purpose and fulfilling enlightened self-interest in an era of expanding access to college for all students, some of whom are not college-ready.

As the aforementioned book title suggests, colleges need to be ready for all students, including those who struggle. Part of this mandate requires shifting from a culture where we expect students to conform to institutions rather than meeting them where they're at. Stephens, Fryberg, Markus, Johnson, and Covarrubias (2012) provide a powerful example of this notion in their findings on the cultural mismatch between universities that tend to promote middle class notions of independence and students from communities where interdependence is more emphasized. This mismatch often manifests in subtle forms, such as institutional messages that students should "find their passion" and "chart their own course." These are not negative ideas. When they are presented as objective reality rather than a perspective among many possible worldviews, however, they can inadvertently alienate students for whom they feel incongruent. As one student explained in a story about her academic advisor, "She wants me to be independent and to figure out what I want to do on my own, but I went to her for guidance and support" (p. 1194).

One might be tempted to read the student's words as coming from a coddled youth, but that seems unlikely given that this scholarship focuses on low income students who are not the students being raised with helicopter parents (Lareau, 2011). We create a false binary when we insist that providing the kind of guidance the aforementioned student craves is antithetical to adult development. I see students who want advice as good researchers; they are both mature and humble enough to draw on the knowledge of those around them. Instead of judging these students, why not honor the vulnerability they show in coming to us with a spirit of openness?

CONCLUSION

I began this book by describing Trump's election in 2016 as the impetus for my entry into the Teaching English as a Foreign Language program at my university. As I sit here writing the conclusion to this book in 2018, the Trump Administration is separating migrant children from their parents under its "Zero Tolerance" policy. That now iconic photograph of the toddler crying for her family peppers my various social media feeds. When I pause on video links of the detention centers, I hear the sobs of children begging for parents.

Like many people in both the days immediately following the 2016 Presidential election and now, I became overwhelmed by the endless hate. Formerly a news junkie, I started to tune it all out. In retrospect, I can see that I was making a decision to give up on structural change because that seemed impossible. I shifted my scholarly agenda from topics like advocacy and activism to mental health and learning. If I couldn't do anything about systems, maybe I could direct my energy toward individuals. This book was born out of that impulse to focus more on what could be gained by understanding thought and feeling more deeply.

What I learned is that being in touch with the human experience is a vital part of positive social change. This revelation may be clearer in its negative form: being out of touch with the human experience is what allows people to treat others callously. The situation is obviously more dire and consequential in the case of migrant children than college students, but the logic is the same. People become problems to be solved or issues to be dealt with when dehumanization creeps into our mindset.

This impulse to treat human concerns as administrative tasks dominates higher education today. Despite the well-crafted communication designed to give the impression of a personalized experience, contemporary college students often do not receive the mentorship and guidance they should. Instead, they are directed toward "resources" for mass produced and overly general advice. Students do sometimes manage to connect with a caring human being, but this individual is very likely helping the student in spite of, not because of, the university bureaucracy. This bureaucracy tends to limit human and financial investment in care work while prioritizing expenditures that can easily be measured.

Although it seems intuitive that investing in struggling students would lead to greater retention, the challenges in measuring the messy process of learning have caused higher education leaders to conceptualize this human condition issue as an administrative problem.

We can't effectively address a problem before we understand it. We've taken the administrative approach to struggling students for years, measuring them and categorizing them and labeling them as specimens. This is not lost on the human beings who must wear these labels. As one student defined as "at-risk" put it, "I refuse to be another statistic and placed in a category no one wants to be in" (Gray, 2013, p. 1249). I was at a conference recently where a researcher created the title of her presentation from a student's assertion that "No one wants to be a loser." Both my students and the ones I read about consistently remind me of the true harm that results from being classified in this way. This is the destructive consequence of approaching struggling students as issues to be assessed rather than humans to be nurtured.

At the height of my struggling student experience, I never had to worry about being labeled "at risk" or a "loser". But even brushing up against those labels for a moment helped me to imagine what the fear of that feels like. That fear did not help or inspire me in any way. What helped and inspired me were the people who chose to be in the struggle with me. We need some fairly monumental change in higher education, but we don't have to wait for it to wade into the struggle with the students in front of us right now. We don't have to do it perfectly; we can be tentative and unsure and riddled with self-doubt. All they will notice is whether or not we're there beside them.

REFERENCES

Astin, A., & Astin, H. (1999). *Meaning and spirituality in the lives of college faculty: A study of value, authenticity, and stress.* Higher Education Research Institute (HERI) Monograph. Los Angeles: University of California.

Bain, K. (2011). *What the best college teachers do.* Cambridge, MA: Harvard University Press.

Berg, M., & Seeber, B. (2016). *The slow professor: Challenging the culture of speed in the academy.* Toronto, ON: University of Toronto Press.

Boyer, E. L., Moser, D., Ream, T. C., & Braxton, J. M. (2015). *Scholarship reconsidered: Priorities of the professoriate.* San Francisco, CA: Wiley.

Braskamp, L. A., Trautvetter, L. C., & Ward, K. (2016). *Putting students first: How colleges develop students purposefully.* San Francisco, CA: Wiley.

Chickering, A. W. (2003). Reclaiming our soul: Democracy and higher education. *Change: The Magazine of Higher Learning, 35*(1), 38–44.

Csikszentmihalyi, M. (2008). *Flow: The psychology of optimal experience.* New York, NY: HarperCollins.

Darley, J. M., & Batson, C. D. (1973). "From Jerusalem to Jericho": A study of situational and dispositional variables in helping behavior. *Journal of Personality and Social Psychology, 27*(1), 100–108.

Di Domenico, S., & Ryan, R. (2017). Primary emotional systems and personality: An evolutionary perspective. *Frontiers in Psychology, 8,* 1414.

Dowland, D., & Pérez, A. (2018, September 23). How to be a generous professor in precarious times. *Chronicle of Higher Education.* Retrieved from https://www.chronicle.com/article/How-to-Be-a-Generous-Professor/244581/.

Duncheon, J. (2015). Making sense of contested terrain: Writing remediation, faculty perspectives, and the challenge of implementation. In W. Tierney & J. Duncheon (Eds.), *The problem of college readiness* (pp. 143–178). Albany, NY: SUNY Press.

Fischer, K. (2016, January 17). Engine of inequality. *Chronicle of Higher Education.* Retrieved from https://www.chronicle.com/article/Engine-of-Inequality/234952.

Gray, S. S. (2013). Framing "at risk" students: Struggles at the boundaries of access to higher education. *Children and Youth Services Review, 35*(8), 1245–1251.

Harrison, L. M., & Price, M. H. (2017). *Interrupting class inequality in higher education: Leadership for an equitable future.* New York, NY: Routledge.

Hartman, Y., & Darab, S. (2012). A call for slow scholarship: A case study on the intesification of academic life and its implications for pedagogy. *Review of Education, Pedagogy, and Cultural Studies, 34*(1–2), 49–60.

Hersh, R. H., & Merrow, J. (2015). *Declining by degrees: Higher education at risk.* New York, NY: St. Martin's Press.

Kerr, C. (1963). *The uses of the university.* Cambridge, MA: Harvard University Press.

Kuh, G., Kinzie, J., Schuh, J., Whitt, E., & Associates. (2005). *Student success in college: Creating conditions that matter.* San Francisco, CA: Jossey-Bass.

Lareau, A. (2011). *Unequal childhoods: Class, race, and family life.* Berkeley: University of California Press.

McNair, T., Albertine, S., Cooper, M., McDonald, N., & Major, T. (2016). *Becoming a student-ready college: A new culture of leadership for student success.* San Francisco, CA: John Wiley & Sons.

Mountz, A., Bonds, A., Mansfield, B., Loyd, J., Hyndman, J., Walton-Roberts, M., & Curran, W. (2015). For slow scholarship: A feminist politics of resistance through collective action in the neoliberal university. *ACME: An International E-Journal for Critical Geographies, 14*(4), 1235–1259.

NCES. (2018). *The condition of education 2018*. Retrieved from https://nces. ed.gov/pubsearch/pubsinfo.asp?pubid=2018144.

Palmer, P. J. (2017). *The courage to teach: Exploring the inner landscape of a teacher's life*. San Francisco, CA: Wiley & Sons.

Pope, D. (2008). *Doing school: How we are creating a generation of stressed out, materialistic, and miseducated students*. New Haven, CT: Yale University Press.

Ray, J., & Kafka, S. (2014). Life in college matters for life after college. *Gallup Latest News*. Retrieved from http://k12accountability.org/resources/For-Parents/Life_in_College_Matters_for_Life_After_College.pdf.

Robinson, T. E., & Hope, W. C. (2013). Teaching in higher education: Is there a need for training in pedagogy in graduate degree programs? *Research in Higher Education Journal, 21*, 1–11.

Rogers, C. (1995). *On becoming a person: A therapist's view of psychotherapy*. New York, NY: Houghton Mifflin Harcourt.

Ryan, R., & Deci, E. (2017). *Self-determination theory: Basic psychological needs in motivation and wellness*. New York, NY: Guilford Press.

Shahjahan, R. A. (2015). Being 'lazy' and slowing down: Toward decolonizing time, our body, and pedagogy. *Educational Philosophy and Theory, 47*(5), 488–501.

Stephens, N. M., Fryberg, S. A., Markus, H. R., Johnson, C. S., & Covarrubias, R. (2012). Unseen disadvantage: How American universities' focus on independence undermines the academic performance of first-generation college students. *Journal of Personality and Social Psychology, 102*(6), 1178.

INDEX